We Are the
RANGERS

*The Oral History
of the New York Rangers*

Stan Fischler

TRIUMPH
BOOKS

Library of Congress Cataloging-in-Publication Data

Fischler, Stan, author.
  We are the Rangers : the oral history of the New York Rangers / Stan Fischler.
     pages cm
  ISBN 978-1-60078-867-3 (pbk.)
  1. New York Rangers (Hockey team)—History. 2. Hockey players—Interviews. I. Title.
  GV848.N43F58 2013
  796.962'64067471—dc23
                    2013022121

This book is available in quantity at special discounts for your group or organization. For further information, contact:
Triumph Books LLC
814 North Franklin Street
Chicago, Illinois 60610
(312) 337-0747
www.triumphbooks.com

Printed in U.S.A.
ISBN: 978-1-60078-867-3
Design by Patricia Frey
Photos courtesy of Fischler Hockey Services unless otherwise indicated

To my eternal pal, jazz maven, and Rangers fan Ira Gitler, who— like myself—was a charter member of the Rangers Fan Club in 1950. And to the memory of Stan Saplin, Herb Goren, and Tom Lockhart of the 1940s and 1950s Rangers high command who substantially helped launch my career in the hockey business.

Contents

Foreword by Rod Gilbert   **vii**

Introduction   **xi**

Part I: The Early Days

Frank Boucher: From the Royal Canadian Mounties to the New York Rangers   **3**

Myles J. Lane: From the Rangers to the New York State Supreme Court   **17**

Tom Lockhart: Rangers Business Manager and the Busiest Executive in Hockey   **33**

Gerry Cosby: Rangers Backup Goalie and Equipment King   **49**

Babe Pratt: The Most Colorful Ranger   **55**

Bill Chadwick: The Almost Ranger Who Became a Hall of Fame Referee   **67**

Part II: The Post–World War II Years

Chuck Rayner: The Rangers' First Hall of Fame Goalie   **83**

Camille Henry: The Skinniest Ranger   **87**

Cal Gardner: Instigator of the Biggest Rangers Fight   **93**

Jack McCartan: From the Olympics to the Blueshirts   **101**

Max Bentley: The Dipsy Doodle Dandy From Delisle   **105**

Andy Bathgate: The Best Post-War Right Wing   **111**

Part III: The Boys of Expansion

Glenn Healy: Backup to the Cup   **121**

Alexei Kovalev: The Rapid Russian   **125**

Brian Leetch: The Best of the Backliners   **133**

James Patrick: Wise Man of the Blue Line   **139**

Part IV: The All-Time Most Popular Rangers

Rod Gilbert: Mr. Ranger   **147**

Mark Messier: The Cup Maker   **153**

Wally Stanowski: The Oldest Living Ranger   **159**

Part V: The Present

Henrik Lundqvist: The King of New York   **165**

Ryan Callahan: The Captain   **173**

Dan Girardi: The Defender   **179**

Rick Nash: The Missing Piece   **185**

Derek Stepan: The Future   **189**

Part VI: The Making of a Fan

How I Became a Rangers Fan: Two Oral Histories   **195**

Acknowledgments   **205**

Epilogue: Two Most Emotional Moments, Four Decades Apart   **207**

Foreword

When I made my playoff debut as a Ranger in the spring of 1962 at the old Madison Square Garden, my buddy Stan Fischler already had been covering the Blueshirts for eight years.

He was there at the start of my NHL career, including my first game. He vividly recalls how it all began for me in Manhattan, and so do I.

Coming to New York, directly from the Kitchener Rangers, I was thrust right into a tension-filled series. We were down two games to none after the club had lost the first two games to the Maple Leafs in Toronto.

Defenseman Doug Harvey, who was our player-coach at the time, put me on a line with Johnny Wilson and Dave Balon during my first practice with the big team.

It was a full house at the Garden, 15,925 fans roaring their heads off. The way the Garden was built, with balconies and mezzanines overhanging the ice, you always had the feeling you were in the middle of a boiler factory. It was wild! They soon quieted down for the playing of the "The Star-Spangled Banner," but erupted again when it ended. This wasn't very good for my nervous system. Because it was a playoff game, I was jumpier than before. Maybe a premonition that I was going to be put right into the game gave me the shakes.

I was right. Just as Harvey said, I was sent out on a line with Balon and Wilson. At first I was uneasy. We were skating against a veteran Toronto team with aces such as Frank Mahovlich, Bob Pulford, Dave Keon, and Allan Stanley. These fellows knew the ropes. They'd been in the Stanley Cup playoffs before and they were tough. For the first two periods I made it my business just to try to keep up with them and not get too fancy until I had the feel of the ice and the opposition. I also wanted to be sure that I got used to Balon and Wilson. It wasn't easy to do. This was a wild game; the goals were bouncing in like ping-pong balls over a net and nobody was waiting around for Rod Gilbert to get used to NHL hockey. But as the game progressed, I realized that I was able to keep up with the Maple Leafs and I began getting my scoring chances.

Late in the third period our line was sent on the ice. We outfeinted the Toronto trio who was guarding us and moved over the blue line in the Toronto zone. I captured the puck and, out of the corner of my eye, noticed that Balon was free. I sent the pass directly to him and he shot it past Johnny Bower. We won the game 5–4, and my assist had helped.

My second game was even better. There had been talk that, since we did so well in the last game, our line would be used even more by Coach Harvey. Sure enough, he put us on the ice for the opening faceoff to start the game.

The play was in motion. We moved the puck into the Leafs' end of the ice. Bower was out of position. The puck landed on my stick. Nothing but me and some air behind Bower. I fired the rubber and it hit the twine behind him. I had scored my first NHL goal—at :41 of the first period in the playoffs, no less! I danced around on the ice like a madman and then dived into the net to retrieve the puck. I wanted to save it for my collection, so I skated with it to the Rangers bench and handed it to our trainer, Frank Paice.

The goal filled me with a sense of exuberance, describable only by telling you that it was like being pumped up with several hundred pounds of helium. I was so excited that I felt I would fly right out of the arena unless I kept my mind on the game. That wasn't hard because the Maple Leafs hadn't given up. They counter-attacked and gave our goalie, Gump Worsley, plenty of trouble. Before the period ended, our line again moved the puck into the Toronto zone. Wilson and Balon passed it back and forth like a yo-yo. Then the puck aimed in my direction. As soon as it touched my stick I flipped it past Bower. When the red light went on I couldn't believe it. At 15:46 of the first period we were ahead 2–0. As soon as we returned to the bench I leaned over and asked Muzz Patrick, who was sitting behind me, to do something he may never have done before: "Muzz, do me a favor and give me a pinch. I think I'm dreaming."

Rod Gilbert is presented with the Most Popular Ranger award for the 1964–65 season.

We won the game 4–2. What made the night even more exciting was my pass to Balon, who scored the third and winning goal of the game. That night was by far the biggest thrill of my life up until then. Now the sky was the limit. I began dreaming impossible dreams and wondering just when I would come out of it, hoping always that I wouldn't.

We never did win the series with Toronto but my dreams kept getting better season by season. I had 24 and 25 goals in my second and third seasons. Despite vertebrae surgery, I returned and in 1970–71 I teamed up with my childhood buddy, Jean Ratelle, and Vic Hadfield. Our chemistry was terrific, and in 1971–72 all three of us got 40 goals and we were named the GAG Line, as in "goal a game."

That season was the closest I came to being on a Stanley Cup-winner. We took the Boston Bruins to six games of the Finals but, in the end, we couldn't stop Bobby Orr, who scored the Cup-winner in Game 6.

Still, I have to be pleased to have played almost two decades in the world's greatest league and all of them with the same team, the Blueshirts, something I'll always be proud of. Really, that completed my dream.

During all those years, I've known Stan Fischler as a journalist and a friend. He and Hal Bock helped me write my book, *Goal—My Life on Ice*, and Stan, like me, continues to be part of the Rangers scene. For these reasons alone, he is the right person to have authored this book, *We Are the Rangers*.

Rod Gilbert and Stan Fischler—we are the Rangers!

—Rod Gilbert
New York Rangers, 1960–78
Hockey Hall of Fame inductee, 1982

Introduction

With all due immodesty, I must say that *We Are the Rangers* is a most appropriate title for this book.

After all, I became a distant member of the Blueshirts family at age seven—in 1939—when I saw my first hockey game at Madison Square Garden.

A mere 15 years later—in 1954—I became an *official* Rangers employee at the enormous sum of $50 per week.

I was hired to be the assistant publicist by manager Frank Boucher, although my immediate boss—and the chap who *really* wanted me on the roster—was Herb Goren, the chief publicist and former baseball and hockey writer for the defunct *New York Sun* newspaper.

Over the intervening decade-and-a-half, from 1939 through 1954, I assiduously worked my way into a paying position with the Rangers, but it was a long, convoluted trail.

My original favorite National Hockey League team was not the Rangers; it was the Toronto Maple Leafs and it remained so until 1951 when my favorite player, defenseman Bashin' Bill Barilko, died in a plane crash a few months after scoring the Stanley Cup–winning goal for Toronto against the Montreal Canadiens.

I was not only stunned to the very core by Barilko's departure; I was equally dismayed when the Leafs high command picked a former schoolteacher named Hugh Bolton to replace my hard-hitting hero.

By sheer, fortuitous coincidence, Boucher and Goren were brainstorming about ways and means to encourage fan support and came up with the absolutely brilliant idea of organizing a Rangers Fan Club, which they did.

Too bad they didn't consult me. A few years earlier, I had joined The Blue Line Club, otherwise known as ardent supporters of the Rangers farm club, the New York Rovers, which played matinees every Sunday at the Garden. No shabby outfit, this. The Blue Liners, led by a chap named Howard Frank, did things right.

They sponsored road trips to venues such as Atlantic City; they put on a very professional song-and-dance end-of-season show for players and fans; and, best of all, they welcomed a young hockey nut like me. With that experience, I became a valued member of the Rangers Fan Club and that included co-editing a monthly mimeograph journal called *The Rangers Review*.

Among other assets, the *Review* enabled me—along with such noble associates as Jerry Weiss and Fred Meier—to actually interview players in person, which we did as avidly as you can imagine.

One of my most vivid memories was an interview Meier and Yours Truly conducted with Rangers forward Ed Kullman. He was staying at the Hotel Belvedere on 49th Street across from the old Garden, resting before a game that night. Kullman was in bed as we hurled question after question at him.

Eddie obliged, being the gentleman that he was (except on the ice, as Rocket Richard would attest), and made it so easy for us that the Meier-Fischler tandem was off and running as hockey journalists.

On the political side, I managed to finagle my way up to the Fan Club's vice presidency, a position I would later use to write two stinging letters to then-NHL president Clarence Campbell. After all, I represented 500 Fan Club members and we strongly resented Campbell's handling of the Geoffrion-Murphy incident in the 1953–54 season.

In a nutshell, what happened was that Boom Boom Geoffrion, then a Canadiens star, nearly killed youthful Rangers forward Ron Murphy with a baseball swing with his stick to Murph's head. The Blueshirts prospect survived with a broken jaw while Campbell's penalties were virtually equal. In my letter I demanded that Campbell further punish Geoffrion.

Gentleman that he was, the NHL president replied with a formal letter that essentially told me to go fly a kite!

No problem. By this time I had my foot in the Rangers office door. In addition to my chores with the *Review* and the Fan Club, I arranged during my senior year at Brooklyn College to be empty of classes on Fridays so that I could do more hockey writing at MSG. This time I approached the Blueshirts business manager, Tom Lockhart, who also ran the Eastern Hockey League and the Rovers as well.

I offered to write—gratis, of course—a weekly newsletter for his Eastern League that could be distributed to all the fans. Lockhart agreed, and I was off and running, writing and delivering the newsletter to the Rangers offices every Friday. Better still, Herb Goren got wind of it, took due note that I reminded him of himself, Goren, at the same age (21), and filed the thought in the back of his cranium.

My next step was yet another case of incredibly lucky timing, thanks to a note informing me that it was time to visit with my college faculty advisor. His name was William Pitt and—no kidding—he was a direct descendent of the William Pitt of Pittsburgh and Pennsylvania fame.

The first thing Professor Pitt wanted to know was what my occupation ambition was at that moment. I respectfully replied that I wanted a job in hockey.

"Did you say *hockey*?" Pitt shot back. I cheerfully repeated my wish.

At that moment, Pitt picked up his telephone and called Stan Saplin, who just happened to be the Rangers beat writer for the *New York Journal-American* newspaper. It was Hearst's flagship evening daily in North America. Prior to his stint at the *J-A*, Saplin had been Goren's predecessor as PR man for the Rangers. Within seconds, Pitt had arranged for me to have lunch with Saplin at the paper's South Street office in the shadow of the Brooklyn Bridge.

Saplin ordered me a cup of coffee in the *J-A*'s cafeteria and then proceeded to tell me, "Stay outta hockey." I couldn't believe my ears but Stan's point was that I should diversify. I insisted that I wanted hockey more than anything. As it happened, Saplin was one of those who helped me get the Rangers job; second assist to William Pitt.

I graduated from Brooklyn College in 1954 and became a member of the Blueshirts organization in September of that year. To say that I had lived a dream come true would be battering a bromide right through the ice. Then again, all my years of scrapbook-collecting, reading—and learning from— endless hockey stories, and the Fan Club writing experience all had paid off at the rate of $50 per week.

My year as a junior press agent for the Rangers was all I hoped it to be except for the fact that we had a losing team and missed the playoffs by a mile-and-a-half. No matter; every day and night I was meeting hockey people, networking (although that word was not known then), and planning to be a Rangers employee for life even though I was furloughed for the summer. But a couple of significant events would change all that.

For one thing, Stan Saplin, who had become my mentor, left the *Journal-American* to become a public relations executive for New York University. His job as Rangers beat writer was filled by Dave Anderson, who had been writing a column about Brooklyn–Long Island sports. Saplin urged me to replace Anderson but I didn't want to leave the Rangers. During August of 1955, I huddled with Goren at an Automat cafeteria on 42nd Street and explained the situation. I was hoping that he'd urge me to come back to the Rangers, but being a wise newspaperman at heart, Herbie knew that the *J-A* offered a terrific opportunity for me as a sports journalist.

I took his advice but managed to stay involved with the Rangers by covering the Blueshirts for *The Hockey News.* And when Anderson moved from the *Journal-American* to *The New York Times,* I got the Rangers beat and held it until the *Journal* merged in 1966 with the *World-Telegram* and *Herald-Tribune.* By then my wife, Shirley, and I took over the New York Bureau of *The Toronto Star* and I continued my coverage of the Blueshirts.

Eventually, I made my way into hockey broadcasting on television and, lo and behold, I'm now back where I started: an employee of Madison Square Garden Network, even reporting on the Rangers from time to time.

Apart from raising a family, hockey has been my life and so have the Blueshirts. Hence *We Are the Rangers* could not be a more natural enterprise for a guy who originally went to work for the team 59 years ago.

When I decided to write about the team that I grew up knowing as the Broadway Blueshirts, I had an assortment of thoughts, some of which had to be deleted for space purposes.

The title itself—*We Are the Rangers*—connotes more than just the fellows who scored the goals and stopped the pucks. I have found during more than a half-century covering the team that some of the most interesting characters were those in the front office and those who even picked out the sticks for the shooters. Gerry Cosby was a good case in point, as you will see.

My fascination with the team's history magnified during the year I worked at the Garden in publicity. One day I discovered, far in the recesses of a long closet, a collection of skates and hockey sweaters.

Since I had been playing ice hockey for fun in those days, I pulled out some of the skates just to see what they were all about. Each pair had a name on it and I soon realized that the skates belonged to players on the 1940 Stanley Cup winners.

In those days the skate of choice was called a CCM Tackaberry. The Tackaberry part related to the Australian kangaroo leather, which then was used as part of the skate boot.

Out of curiosity I picked out several skates to see if my feet could fit in them. After several tries the skate that belonged to Dutch Hiller fit perfectly. I took the pair home and later had them sharpened at the Brooklyn Ice Palace by a fellow named Tubby Ensign, who was amazed that the blade still had enough steel left to be used for at least a year or two. And so they were, although I hardly scored as many goals as Hiller did during his halcyon days as a Ranger.

Having worked in an office so reeking with history, I couldn't help but learn about other fascinating aspects of New York's NHL lore. One of the other finds in that endless closet was a white-and-red sweater that belonged to the Springfield Indians. It so happened that Springfield was a farm team in the American Hockey League of the New York Americans and this jersey was worn by Hall of Famer Eddie Shore when he bought the club late in 1930 and actually skated occasionally for the Indians.

Over the years fellows such as Tommy Lockhart—who wore more hats than anyone in hockey—fed me stories about their colorful past. Cal Gardner actually told me the story about how he fought with Ken Reardon when the latter was a defenseman for the Montreal Canadiens.

One of my favorite stories was another of Gardner's, only this time from when he was a member of the Boston Bruins and actually "talked" the Rangers out of a playoff berth by virtue of a conversation with then-Ranger Max Bentley. You'll have to read the Gardner chapter to understand how that happened.

Equally dear to me is the Wally Stanowski chapter. This germinated from a visit to the Gerry Cosby Sporting Goods store many years ago. The owner, Gerry's son Mike, mentioned that he had gone to college with Stanowski's son Skip, who was an excellent university hockey player.

What's more he put me in touch with Skip, who in turn connected me with his illustrious father, who played on several Stanley Cup–winning teams in Toronto. Yet Wally confessed to me that his most enjoyable hockey experience was with the Rangers.

I'm tickled that Wally, at 94 years old, is still hale and hearty, living in Toronto. He remains the oldest living Ranger, and his contribution to the book, although it only covers a couple of seasons in New York, is very meaningful to me. Let's not forget that Stanowski played on the 1949–50 Blueshirts who came within an inch of winning the Stanley Cup in a seven-game series with the Detroit Red Wings.

More recently I've been able to meet Rangers of recent eras and occasionally work on television with the likes of Brian Leetch, Mike Keenan, and Ron Duguay, each of whom has woven many a delightful hockey tale to me.

If I share one thing in common with all these characters involved it has been a love of hockey, and I hope you enjoy this work.

Part I
The Early Days

chapter one

Frank Boucher

From the Royal Canadian Mounties to the New York Rangers

BORN: Ottawa, Ontario, October 7, 1901

DIED: December 12, 1977

POSITION: Center, Ottawa Senators, 1921–22; New York Rangers, 1926–44; Coach, New York Rangers, 1939–49, 1953–54; General Manager, New York Rangers, 1948–55

AWARDS/HONORS: Lady Byng Memorial Trophy, 1927–31, 1932–35; NHL Second Team All-Star, 1931; NHL All-Star, 1932–35; Hockey Hall of Fame, 1958

Frank Boucher enjoyed one of the longest runs with one team in NHL history.

Nicknamed "Raffles" (a fictional safecracker) because of Boucher's deft stick-handling skills that seemed capable of breaking into the most difficult safes, he signed with the Rangers in 1926, the club's first year in the National Hockey League, and eventually became coach of the 1940 Stanley Cup–winning team and later general manager after the retirement of Lester Patrick. Thus his career spanned 29 years including two Stanley Cups in 1928 and 1933.

My introduction to Boucher would not come until the early 1950s while I was a student at Brooklyn College and vice president of the Rangers Fan Club. After graduation, I was appointed assistant publicist for the club and Boucher was my boss.

He gave me a handsome salary of $50 per week, later hiked to $55 in midseason. Boucher liked me and I loved him like a favorite uncle. In addition to his *smarts, "Boosh," as we all called him, was a jocular fellow who annually starred with Joseph Nichols of The New York Times. The pair would do a delightful Vaudeville song and dance act to the tune, "Are You From Dixie."*

To this day, the vignette of Boosh and Joe Nick doing their routine is one of my favorite memories.

The good news was that during the 1954–55 season, I was able to spend considerable time schmoozing with Boucher; from those chats our friendship tightened and I was able to record many of his tales. The bad news was at the end of the season I was stunned to the core when Boucher was fired and replaced by our then-coach Murray Patrick, the younger son of Lester Patrick.

Boucher later became active in Junior hockey in Western Canada, and we remained in touch. Frank died on December 12, 1977, at the age of 76. It could be argued that Boucher was the greatest Ranger of them all, but that's not the point. The point is that he was my favorite as player, coach, and general manager.

Our oral history begins with Boucher talking about his start as a professional player in the Roarin' Twenties:

Are you kidding? Get a bonus for signing my NHL contract? Not on your life.

Back in 1921 that's the way it was. Attitudes were different then. We didn't have the agents, attorneys, and what-have-you that the Bobby Orrs and Bobby Hulls had later. When the Ottawa Senators asked me to play for them in 1921 I signed a one-year contract for $1,200 and considered myself very lucky and happy to be playing hockey. Nobody cared about images and stuff like that. It's not that way anymore though; today, hockey players are all business. Why, I once heard that Phil Esposito got paid for a one-hour speaking engagement what I got paid for a whole season! Imagine that. And here I won the Lady Byng Trophy seven times and never made more than $8,500 in one season.

Of course, we didn't have a players' association in our day and weren't wrapped up in all those other trappings. Frankly, I don't know whether it was dedication to the sport or if we were just damn fools. But there's one thing I'm sure of—I know we had a heck of a lot more fun than they do today. That's where we had it over them, in the laughs.

I'll never forget that first Rangers training camp. It was the fall of 1926 and Conn Smythe, our manager, had booked us into the Peacock Hotel, which was right on the outskirts of Toronto. Smythe was later replaced by Lester Patrick but at that time he was organizing the club and he was a real stickler for discipline. One of the things he did was set an early curfew. That was fine except that I had been out having a good time with Ching Johnson and by the time we got back to the hotel that night the place was completely locked.

No matter how hard we tried we couldn't get into the place, so we decided to do the next best thing and head for a hotel downtown. Since there were no cabs around we walked a few blocks to an intersection and discovered a trolley car about to start its first run of the morning. It was about 6:00 AM when we got on the trolley and the motorman was an awfully friendly chap. We offered him a bit of the applejack we had been drinking and he proved to be a very congenial host.

After about 10 minutes he said he had to start the trolley on its run and asked, "Where are you gentlemen going?" I told him we'd like to head for the King Edward Hotel but at the time I didn't realize it wasn't exactly on the same route as the trolley normally would go. The motorman said he'd oblige and before you could say "Jack Robinson" he turned off all the lights except those up front and started downtown.

We had gone about three blocks when we came to the first trolley station where a half-dozen or so people were waiting to get on, but our man didn't slow one bit; he just plowed straight ahead as if the only thing that mattered was getting us to the King Edward Hotel.

We passed enough passengers in a mile or so that somebody surely must have phoned the Toronto Transit Commission to complain, but as I said our motorman didn't seem to care—at least not until we reached a corner where there was a switch. At that point he must've realized the tracks weren't going to take us to the King Edward even though his route was supposed to go directly ahead.

Suddenly he gets one of those big steel rods, runs out onto the tracks, and pulls the switch, and off we go toward the hotel. By this time the three of us made quite a barber shop trio and were singing every good song in the book until we looked up and saw the King Edward ahead. Our friend stopped the trolley directly in front of the hotel, shook our hands, and then took off into the early morning.

I was associated with the Rangers for 28 years as a player, coach, and manager and I can say without hesitation that the 1927–28 New York team and the 1939–40 team were the best Rangers clubs of all time and among the finest ever seen in the NHL. Naturally, I'm a little partial to the 1927–28 team because I played on it and I was in my prime then. What made it so great was its two very strong lines—in those day we didn't have a three- or four-line system as they do today—plus a defense that no club could equal and good goalkeeping. You knew we were good because we won the Cup in strange circumstances.

We couldn't play any of the final Cup games in New York then because Madison Square Garden had other commitments, so all our "home" games had to be played on the road, making it tremendously difficult. We eliminated Pittsburgh and Boston in the opening rounds, then went up against the Montreal Maroons and had to play all the games at the Montreal Forum.

That was the series where our regular goalie, Lorne Chabot, got hurt and old Lester Patrick went into the nets. From my own standpoint that was unforgettable because I scored the winning goal at 7:05 of sudden death. Unfortunately, the Maroons were up 2–1 in wins but I scored the only goal in the fourth game and we took it 1–0. So it all boiled down to the fifth game since it was a best-of-five series.

After Lester went in as goalie and we won, we got Joe Miller to goaltend for us. He'd been nicknamed "Red Light" Miller because he played for the Americans and they were losers at that time. I personally never thought he was bad, and as things turned out, he was terrific in that last game. Right off the bat we were behind the eight ball. We got a penalty and I was sent out to try to kill the clock until our man returned. For quite a few seconds we did pretty well and then somebody got the puck to me and I found myself at center ice, skating in on Red Dutton, a Maroon defenseman. I knew Red's weakness—if you pushed the puck through his legs he'd give his attention to it instead of watching you. I tried the trick and, sure enough, he looked down. By the time he looked up I was around him and had picked up the puck, skated in on their goalie, Clint Benedict, and flipped it into the right-hand corner.

Not very long after that we got hit with another penalty and Lester sent me out again. My only concern was to stickhandle the puck as much as possible at center ice; however, I suddenly found myself in a position where my only

Frank Boucher (7) in front of the Toronto net.

play was to shoot the puck off the boards and hope to pick up the rebound and keep possession. I miscalculated and shot the puck so far ahead that Dunc Munro, the Maroons defenseman, thought he could intercept it.

The puck was about midway between Munro and me, and as I watched him, I realized he was going to try to beat me to it. He came on for quite a run and I could almost hear him thinking, *By God, I can't get there quite in time*. He seemed to stop in one motion, then change his mind and go for the puck again. All the while, I was skating madly toward it, and by this time I had reached it. I just swooped over to one side and let Munro go by; I had the whole ice to myself, straight to the goaltender.

I moved directly in on Benedict and landed a goal in almost the exact place as I did earlier. We won the game 2–1 and the Cup. It certainly was a tribute to Lester; if he hadn't gone into the nets when Chabot was hurt I don't know what we would have done. But that was Lester: a very, very interesting man and a tough taskmaster as well.

One funny story about Lester Patrick stands out. We had played in Ottawa one night and won the game with some fantastic score like 10–1 and we went to a party afterward in Hull, Quebec, the town across the river. I guess we stayed long past our curfew but initially decided it was time to get back our Pullman sitting in the Ottawa station. We all knew that Lester must have been asleep so we tiptoed onto the train and kept passing the word along in whispers: "Don't wake Lester!"

It seemed to us that we managed to sneak in without disturbing him—or so I thought until the next morning when I walked into the diner for breakfast. Lester, who was sitting there alone, looked up and said, "Good morning, Mr. Boucher." As soon as he called me by my last name I knew something was wrong. I sat down next to him and nothing was said for about a minute until Lester offhandedly mentioned to me, "Did you know that Butch Keeling walks in his sleep?"

I said, "No, Lester, I didn't." To which Lester replied, "Y'know, Frank, that's very interesting because at about 4:00 in the morning Butch walked into my compartment, peed on the floor, and whispered something about 'Don't wake Lester!'"

There wasn't much I could say after that but if you think I was tongue-tied then let me tell you about another situation that really put me on the hot seat for quite some time. It occurred during the 1930–31 season. Cecil Dillon joined the Rangers as a rookie and it didn't take long for me to discover I was his idol, but not just as a hockey player.

Cecil had been crazy about the Royal Canadian Mountain Police ever since he was a kid, and when he found out that I had once been a Mountie there was nothing I could do to discourage him. It became embarrassing because I was only a Mountie for a short time, as all the other Rangers knew, and had never served in any of the wild Northwest outposts. Dillon nevertheless began to press me about my experiences. At first I thought I'd just let him know that nothing much really had happened to me but I could tell that he was really keen to hear something so I began with a few honest-to-goodness yarns of incidents that actually did occur. They were my best true stories and I hoped they'd be sufficient.

I didn't know whether to be happy or sad about it but Dillon thought my stories were just the greatest things in the world and began begging me to tell some more. Unfortunately, I ran out of true stories and had to make a decision: either let on to Dillon that absolutely nothing else happened that was interesting or start fabricating stories. My mistake was in deciding to do everything possible to make the rookie happy. The next time we sat down I told him a whole pile of fictitious tales.

You name it, I did it. Boucher battled the Indians; Boucher commanded a dog team in the Arctic; Boucher was all over the Northwest. When my imagination ran dry I went to the nearest newsstand to pick up a few Western magazines to restore my supply. After a while I even began to hope that Lester might trade Cecil, just to get him off my back. That didn't happen, though; Dillon was an awfully good hockey player and just as nice a guy to boot. His problem was that he kept wanting more Mountie stories and I had to keep telling them.

Once and only once I was nearly exposed. The Rangers were in Atlantic City for some reason and several of us took a stroll on the Boardwalk. When we passed a shooting gallery Dillon asked me to join him in a few rounds, figuring that as a former Mountie my shooting would be super. Actually, I couldn't shoot the side of a barn.

Cecil started shooting first and he was deadly accurate. He had done quite a bit of hunting back home in Ontario so this was second nature to him. When he got through he handed me the gun and I couldn't touch a thing—not one bloody target! It reached such a point that I could tell Cecil was wearing a long face because he was horrified at my performance.

I was about to let on to him that I had been telling a pack of fibs when I suddenly thought of something. I took Cecil aside and mentioned that while he was firing at the targets I had spoken to the fellow running the gallery and had told him to put blanks in my rifle. Cecil fell for it and as long as he played for the Rangers he remained convinced of all those Mountie tales.

Maybe that helped me later when I became the Rangers manager, because we needed all the imagination we could get during those bad years. But they didn't come until later; we had some marvelous teams in the 1930s. After I retired and was made coach we had a wonderful bunch of boys in the 1939–40 season. Yes, that was one of the greatest teams in history.

Tops in every position: it started with Davey Kerr in goal; Art Coulter and Murray Patrick as one defense team; and Babe Pratt and Ott Heller on the other. The three forward lines were just fantastic: Phil Watson–Bryan Hextall–Lynn Patrick; Neil and Mac Colville–Alex Shibicky; and Clint Smith–Kilby MacDonald–Alf Pike, with Dutch Hiller as the spare. They were perfect players for a coach because you could encourage suggestions and they'd always come up with something good that we'd practice and eventually use in a game. One result was the "box defense," where the four players killing a penalty arranged themselves in a box formation in front of the goalkeeper. We had another strategy called offensive penalty-killing which turned out to be the beginning of the modern forechecking. In this one, we tried for goals when we were a man short instead of going into a defensive shell. We'd send out three forwards and one defenseman and we'd forecheck in their own end. Our team was so good it scored more goals over a season than it had goals scored upon it during penalty-killing. Once, though, it backfired on us.

We had perfected this system—or so we thought—and went into Chicago with a 19-game unbeaten streak. In that 20th game we played rings around the Black Hawks and should have won by a big margin but for some strange reason we couldn't score a goal. We were down 1–0 into the third period.

During intermission we were batting around ideas in the dressing room when the guys came up with another new one. It was decided that if we were still down by a goal in the final minute of play we'd pull the goalkeeper and send out an extra skater. Up until that point, the way the system worked you never put the extra man on the ice until there was a whistle for a faceoff. But we thought it'd be better not to make it obvious that we were pulling the goalie; in other words, do it on the fly while the play was still going on. That was the plan.

I made one big mistake; I forgot to tell Lester our plan, and on this particular night he was sitting on our bench, which he rarely did in those days. Toward the end of the game, though, he walked over to the Chicago Stadium timekeeper because he didn't trust him and wanted to keep an eye on the clock.

We still were down a goal and the puck was in the opposition's end of the rink. This was the time to try the new plan and the signal was given for Davey Kerr to come off the ice and for the extra forward to go on. That's exactly what happened and nobody in the rink knew what was going on except my players—and then Lester. But he didn't realize that Kerr was removed from the goal. So Lester had thought I made a mistake and put too many men on the ice and started screaming for me to take the "extra" man off before we got a penalty. Paul Thompson, the Black Hawks coach, heard him, and when he saw six men in his zone he started screaming, too. Meanwhile, we had moved the puck into scoring position and the plan was working perfectly. We were about to put it in the net when the referee blew his whistle to give us a penalty. Then he turned around, saw that Kerr was out, and realized there shouldn't be a penalty at all. But it was too late. The attack was stopped and we lost the game.

As things turned out we won the next five games in a row for an overall record of 24 wins or ties in 25 games and went on to win the Stanley Cup. Then the war came and we lost most of our really good players; when it was over a lot of them came back but they had lost a step or two and weren't really the same. That's when we had to start rebuilding, which took quite some time. And naturally, when times were bad we used to resort to all kinds of tricks to get people into the Garden.

There was one period during the war years when things hit an all-time low. We had lost such fellows as Jim Henry, Murray Patrick, Art Coulter, and Alex Shibicky to the armed forces, and by the time October of 1942 came around,

Frank Boucher skates with the puck against the Bruins in November 1931.

more than half our roster that had finished first the previous spring was gone. It was time for training camp to start, and believe it or not, we didn't have a goalkeeper on hand, not one! Lester was just as worried as I was and I told him the only thing we could do was to check out every town in Canada to see if we could find one. We sent telegrams to all our scouts telling them to wire us if they came across a goalie, and three days later, we got word from our man in Saskatchewan, Al Ritchie. He said he had a chap named Steve Buzinski who'd play goal for us and so I told Ritchie to get him to our camp immediately.

Camp was in Winnipeg, as it had been for years, and when we got there and started workouts I discovered that nobody named Buzinski had arrived.

Well, there was nothing much we could do but sit around and hope that he'd show up; meanwhile we sent the boys through the practice skates and light workouts. After a day or so I really began to get worried but on this particular afternoon we were on the ice when I looked over toward the sideboards and got the surprise of my life.

In the Winnipeg Amphitheater the sideboards were quite a bit higher than in other rinks, and as I looked at them I saw this tiny fellow walking along, wearing a black helmet—but all I could see was the helmet over the side-boards. I first thought that it was a "rink rat," one of those lads who hangs around the rink and cleans the ice between workouts. But soon I saw one goalie pad, then another, climb over the boards, and sure enough, this little chap skated directly to the net. I remember saying to myself when I looked at him, "Oh my gosh, it can't be *him*!"

This was Steve Buzinski; he not only was small but he was also bow-legged and when he stood in front of the net you saw nothing but holes. We didn't have much choice, since there were no other goalkeepers around, so Steve was our man when the 1942–43 season started. I can't say he was the greatest but he did try and he had a strange sense of humor. One night we were playing in Detroit and the Red Wings were scoring on him left and right. Sometime late in the game one of the Detroit players took a long shot and Buzinski nabbed it in his glove and casually tossed it aside, as though he were a Vezina Trophy winner. Just as he did, one of our boys skated by and heard Steve say: "Y'know, this is as easy as picking cherries off a tree!"

I can't honestly say our losing was entirely Steve's fault but when we found out there was another goalie available with more experience—Jimmy Franks—we got him, but kept Buzinski on the payroll because he was good for his humor and in those days we needed all the humor we could get. Lester finally got rid of him after he refused to attend a practice with our farm team, the Rovers. I believe he told Lester he had some letters to write home and that's all Lester needed. Buzinski was on the next train to Saskatchewan.

The fun didn't end with Steve. We had some lulus after the war too. Remember Dr. David Tracy, the hypnotist we brought in to help the team win? That was when we were running into tough luck again, in the early 1950s. Tracy was a big bloke who thought he could give the Rangers a winning complex. The night of a Bruins game he talked to Buddy O'Connor and a few of the other players and then they went out and lost the game in the final minute. We didn't see much of Dr. Tracy after that but it wasn't the end of the gimmicks. Gene Leone, the owner of Mamma Leone's Restaurant, tried to help us once with what he called "a magic elixir." He concocted some combination of clam juice or broth and a few other items, put it into a big black bottle, and offered it to the boys in the hopes it would get us going.

It worked a lot better than Dr. Tracy had and we actually started winning after Gene created it. Pretty soon the black bottle became a thing around town and Jim Burchard, who was covering hockey for *The World-Telegram*, decided we should also take it on our road trips. We had a Saturday night game in Toronto and Jim took a plane there, bottle in hand.

Damned if we didn't beat the Maple Leafs 4–2. Now, everybody's talking about Leone's black bottle and wondering what's in it. I don't think Gene expected to become so popular, and since he was a busy man, he wasn't able to brew it every time. Once, we didn't have the magic elixir and we lost to the Red Wings. Burchard claimed that without the bottle we were at a psychological disadvantage.

After a while, bottle or not, we got into the old rut and eventually finished in fifth place, out of the playoffs. That was the end of the era of the magic elixir. Of course, my hope was to fill the Garden because we had a good hockey team, not a gimmick. At the same time, I was always trying to think of ways to improve the game. One of my ideas was the use of two goaltenders on a team instead of one. I was a good 20 years before my time since it's standard practice today, but in the late 1940s it was somewhat revolutionary.

At that time, I had two good goalkeepers: "Sugar" Jim Henry and Charlie Rayner. Not only were they teammates, but they were also good friends off the ice and it was always a tough decision whenever I'd have to consider which one to play. I decided to alternate them during the game so I started to change goaltenders every five minutes and it worked. Except I ran into an odd thing once against Toronto when there was only one pair of gloves for them both to use and every time they passed each other during a change they'd transfer gloves, which looked kind of funny at the time.

They both lasted with us for a while until we got rid of Henry, though we kept Rayner. Charlie was a good goaltender who helped take us to the Stanley Cup Finals in 1950. But then things got rough again.

By 1953–54 we had a horrible hockey team and I had to figure out how to keep the fans from dropping off. That's when I signed Max Bentley and later talked his older brother, Doug, into coming to New York, even though they both were past their prime.

I got Max at the start of the season and he still was good, but a funny sort of character. He was a hypochondriac, always carrying boxes of pills around for all his imaginary illnesses. I had a hell of a time just keeping him playing because of some trivial thing that happened to be bothering him at the time. I felt if I could get Doug to play for us as well he'd get Max to do things he wouldn't ordinarily.

Without Doug, I had to pamper Max. We even brought his cousin, Bev, to New York as our spare goaltender, just to try to keep Max happy. The Bentleys believed in traveling together, like a tribe. If you invited them over it was nothing for 12 to 14 Bentleys—the whole shebang—to come along. So I kept after Doug, trying to get him away from Saskatoon where he was player-coach. Phone calls didn't work so I finally decided to fly up to Canada and talk directly to him. It took a while—and a lot of money—but I managed to persuade him to take a fling at it with the Rangers.

It was worth every penny just to see Doug and Max back together again after all those years with Edgar Laprade on the line with them. I remember Coley Hall of the Vancouver team coming all the way from British Columbia just to see the Bentleys together once more. They scored a whole bunch of goals between them and we beat the Bruins; after it was over Hall said, "That was the greatest thing I ever saw."

Personally, I didn't think they'd be sensations right off the bat. But they were fantastic, passing and shooting and skating just like in the old days. Doug was the one who put the desire in Max when Max would lose confidence in himself.

After they teamed up we gave the Bruins a good run for fourth place but Lynn Patrick was coaching Boston at the time and knew what to do to stop them. Realizing that he couldn't make Doug back down, he had his players lay into Max. "As soon as Max goes for the puck," he told them, "you go get him!" They managed to slow Max down but Doug still played beautifully right down to the end. I wish I could say we made the playoffs but it didn't happen that way; we finished fifth.

Just watching those Bentleys convinced me of one thing: the biggest mistake ever made in hockey was breaking up that team, Max and Doug, when they played for Chicago. They were a funny pair of brothers.

While all of this was going on I was trying to build up the farm system, especially the Juniors in Guelph, Ontario. A year after the Bentleys we began to show real progress. Andy Bathgate, Dean Prentice, Harry Howell, and Lou Fontinato all came out of the Guelph Juniors but they were still a little green. We missed the playoffs again in 1954–55, my last season as manager of the Rangers. After that, Guelph kids really developed and the Rangers had a good run of playoff times. It sort of did my heart good to see how they turned out.

chapter two

Myles J. Lane

From the Rangers to the New York State Supreme Court

BORN: Melrose, Massachusetts, October 2, 1905

DIED: August 6, 1987

POSITION: Defenseman, New York Rangers, 1928–29; Boston Bruins, 1929–30, 1933–34

Myles J. Lane easily could have been mistaken for an All-American football player or even a judge rather than an NHL defenseman for the Rangers. That would not come as a surprise to anyone who knew the tall, handsome scholar-athlete. As a gridder, he starred for Dartmouth College's varsity team and would later become an attorney and eventually Justice of the New York State Supreme Court.

He became a member of the Blueshirts in their third season of existence, 1928– 29, and lasted long enough to become the chief protagonist in one of the funniest front office episodes in history. And while he only played part of one season for New York, his saga is so unique—both as an athlete and jurist—it merits a position in this book.

When I met Lane and his wife at their East Side Manhattan apartment, he was 64 years old and still looked like a perfectly formed athlete. Our interview took place in December of 1969, and I still revere the vignette of his gentlemanly deportment and willingness to relate tale after tale of his ventures on ice.

Our oral history begins with Lane recalling his earliest days as a stickhandler in New England.

Lots of places across the United States could qualify as "the hockey capital of the nation" but my choice is Melrose, Massachusetts, my hometown. Even before I grew up, hockey was the number one sport there, and some really fine players learned the game in our neighborhood.

Many people in the States know the name Hobey Baker since he's one of the few Americans in the Hockey Hall of Fame, but we had a fellow in Melrose, "Bags" Wanamaker, who in those days was the next best thing to Baker. He wasn't the only top-notch skater around. Hago Harrington, later a big man in Boston hockey, was also from our area and, like me, played on the big pond in the middle of town whenever it was frozen.

I was about six years old when I got my first pair of skates and it was something awful trying to learn on them. I attempted to play with the big boys but could hardly stand up on the blades and was so small my hockey stick would be taller than I was and end up around the faces of my bigger friends. In other words, I was highsticking at the age of six.

We had hockey little leagues in grammar school then just as they have in Canada and in parts of the United States now. And, don't forget, this was back in the early 1920s.

It took a bit of time but I soon started to improve my skating and when I reached my teens I was good enough to play defense for our high school team. That was really something. Ours was the best hockey team in the state; we won something like 23 games and lost only one during a single season and that was because we were physically exhausted.

I'll tell you just how good we were. We once scrimmaged with Harvard, the intercollegiate champions, and although they beat us 2–1 in a 60-minute game, it was quite a feather in the cap of Melrose High. That same year we defeated Boston College.

Even though I was playing defense for the high school team, I liked rushing and did quite a lot of puck-carrying; I continued to rush right through my college playing career since nobody said, "Don't do it." Meanwhile, I played against some really first-rate competition. When I was still in high school I can remember being permitted to play for a team that took on a bunch passing themselves off as amateurs but who later became the Pittsburgh Yellow Jackets. They were really pros but nobody said anything about it.

All of this gave me terrific experience. Here I was, only 16 years old, going up against fellows who were professionals. It provided quite a head start for my college tryout and, in retrospect, it made playing college hockey as easy as rolling off a log. When it came time for me to select a college, I went up to Hanover, New Hampshire, to look over Dartmouth. I had already received three or four football scholarships elsewhere but liked the looks of Dartmouth and decided to go there, although they didn't give any hockey scholarships.

College hockey was very big in those days. We played Harvard, Yale, Princeton, Toronto, Boston University, and M.I.T. Whenever we played in Boston against Harvard or Yale, the arena would be packed, and usually the proceeds for those games went to a charity.

At the time my heart was set on graduating from Dartmouth and then going to law school. I didn't think I wanted to be a professional athlete for the simple reason that a top-notch hockey player couldn't stay in the NHL for more than eight or 10 years, but one could have a lifetime career by going into law, finance, or some other business.

I also figured only the really big stars made the big money. I knew I was taking something of a gamble but my target was law school, not the NHL. Then, in my senior year, our team went up against the University of Toronto, managed by Conn Smythe, who soon left the university to become boss of the Maple Leafs. Apparently he liked the way I played because he contacted me to say he'd like me to join the Toronto Maple Leafs.

Naturally, I was flattered but I told Smythe I wanted to go to law school; and if I was going to pursue hockey I would do it with a team in the United States. That way, I could continue my law studies and still play hockey. In those days if a representative of an NHL team talked with you it meant your name was automatically put on that team's list and no other team could negotiate with you.

So I wound up with my name on the Toronto Maple Leafs' negotiation list. I've since heard that Boston had wanted to sign me too because I was a local boy—Melrose is only about seven miles outside Boston—but they couldn't deal with me on account of Smythe. After a while I convinced Smythe that I

Myles J. Lane (kneeling, second from left) was a star on the Dartmouth hockey team, which played outdoors until an indoor rink was built in the late 1920s.
(Dartmouth Athletic Communications)

didn't want to go to Toronto, so the Leafs swapped my name with the New York Rangers and Toronto took a player from the New York list.

The Rangers didn't own me; I was still in college and I hadn't signed with them. In fact, I didn't talk to anybody connected with the Rangers until after I had made a trip south that spring with the Dartmouth baseball team. We had gone down to Atlanta and were heading home when I got a wire from Colonel Hammond, the Rangers president. He said he wanted to see me in New York, which was okay with me since we were stopping off at Philadelphia for a game against the University of Pennsylvania.

After the game I went up to New York and sat down with him. The first thing he said was that he wanted me to sign, but I replied, "Nothing doing."

At the time I just wasn't sure that I wanted to go into hockey. There were other things on my mind, other offers.

One was an opportunity to teach at the Taft School in Connecticut, and I couldn't decide whether I wanted to play one year of hockey or teach one year at Taft, then go to law school. I spoke to Mr. Taft and he said something to me I've never forgotten.

"Mr. Lane, the job is yours, if you want it. But don't fool me!"

I asked, "What do you mean?"

He answered, "Don't come here for one year and then leave me. It's a good position if you want to teach for the rest of your life. But don't fool with me. Let me know if you intend to stay with me or just want to make it a one-year proposition."

"Mr. Taft," I told him, "I can't fool you and I can't give you an answer. I have in the back of my head a desire to go into the law business so I'm not certain whether I'd stay one year or more than one."

Right then and there with that exchange I decided to accept the Rangers' hockey proposition. In September, I contacted Colonel Hammond and signed with New York, got a bonus, and made a lot more money than any of my college classmates did.

When I joined the Rangers they had four defensemen led by Ching Johnson and Taffy Abel. The third man was Leo Bourgeault, a little fellow about 5'8" and 140 pounds. Leo was a rushing defenseman but too small to do much checking. I was the fourth man. Strangely enough, coach Lester Patrick started me out with Ching.

I'll never forget my first game at Madison Square Garden. I was thrown off the ice three times with penalties and Ching finally came over to me and said, "If you don't cut this out you're going to be the bad man of hockey instead of me."

But my penalties were the result of inexperience more than anything else; after all, I was just a rookie. Then, after the game, a funny thing happened.

A fellow by the name of Eddie O'Neill was covering hockey for the Associated Press at the time and he came into our dressing room and started interviewing me. His first question was: "How did you feel out there tonight in your first game as a professional?"

I replied, "Well, it wasn't really too bad out there."

Eddie said, "No, give me an angle. Look, I'm like you—I'm a college man. Was there anything different out there from the kind of hockey you experienced at Dartmouth?"

"Look, Eddie," I told him, "that's a silly question because you know as well as I do that there's no comparison between college and professional hockey. It's an entirely different game, like the difference between minor league baseball and major league ball."

O'Neill went on. "Let me ask you a couple of questions," he said. "Did you ever play a college game in which you were a lot more tired than you are tonight?"

I said, "Of course I did," and he asked, why.

"When I played college hockey," I replied, "I played as much as 60 minutes without relief. If you're in a daisy chain for 60 minutes, you'll still get tired of walking around. But out there tonight I'd get relief every three or four minutes so I wasn't so tired afterward."

"Wasn't it rough?" O'Neill asked.

"Sure," I said, "it's rougher than the college game, but I wasn't tired because of the relief I got."

When O'Neill was finished I got dressed, returned to my hotel, and went to bed. The next morning I went downstairs for breakfast and ran into the desk clerk, a friend of mine. He asked if I had seen the *Times* that morning and when I replied "no" he said, "Here, take a look."

So I picked up the paper and saw a headline across the sports page that read, "LANE SAYS PROFESSIONAL HOCKEY A CINCH COMPARED TO THE COLLEGE BRAND."

That was really something. Worse still, I had to report to the Garden later that day, since it was customary to check in with the club on a daily basis. When I walked into the dressing room there were all those Canadian players and me, just an American collegian—and you could have cut the silence with a knife.

I simply told them the headline was a complete fabrication; I had never made such a claim. And that was that as far as the players themselves were concerned.

Not long after, we took a trip to Montreal to play the Maroons. This was the English team that represented Montreal in the NHL, and they were big, husky, and tough. When we arrived in town I picked up a paper and read an article exhorting the populace to come down to the game and watch this upstart American collegian get his comeuppance. The paper went on to say how I had told a reporter what a simple game this Canadian hockey was, and so forth.

As expected, the people came streaming into the Forum that night looking for blood and I knew it. On the very first rush I made down the ice two Maroons came at me and tried to put me right over the sideboards. One of them went off with a penalty.

I rushed down the ice three times and on those three rushes three Montreal players went into the cooler. The game got rougher and rougher as it went along. Later on, Ching Johnson skated down the ice and was whacked hard by one of the Maroons. He lost his balance and slid into the backboards. Though he threw both his feet up to break the slide, unfortunately his skate got caught in the boards and his ankle twisted around and broke. He was through for the season.

After that happened Taffy Abel made a rush down the ice and someone stepped on his foot. He needed 13 stitches to close the wound. That left Leo Bourgeault and myself on defense. We got beaten, and the next night we went to Boston where we again lost. Then it was on to Pittsburgh and a 0–0 tie, followed by a tie with Detroit. That was my introduction to pro hockey, and the reception was all due to some misinformation.

Naturally, I could handle myself out on the ice. I was about 6'1" and 195 pounds and I remembered what Ching had told me at the start: "The first lesson in this game is to protect yourself. Make sure when you bump somebody that your stick is right up in front of you so they don't give you the stick in the face. When you hit them, hit them hard; hit them clean if you can but always protect yourself because in this game there are no medals for bravery."

So whenever I bumped somebody, I remembered Ching's advice and never got into much trouble. I got put off the ice quite a bit but never had to drop my gloves and punch. And, after that first incident, I was never really needled about being a collegian. On the whole the guys were very fair.

When I was with the Rangers my boss was Lester Patrick, a fine man who treated me fairly, there was no question about it. After a while he suggested that I be sent down to Springfield for some polishing up in the minors. And he was right. If I'd been going to make a career of hockey I would have said "yes" and gone to Springfield but I wasn't in it for life; I was in it to get enough money for law school. Of course, the Rangers didn't know that until Lester suggested I go to Springfield. He wanted me there for a month or two and I said I'd go, but on only one condition: that I get my full share of money if the club won the Stanley Cup.

He said he couldn't agree to that and maintained I would have to go down to Springfield. It was February and the season was almost over. "Oh, no," I told Lester, "I don't have to go because if you insist that I do, then I'll just quit hockey."

The next thing I knew I was traded to the Boston Bruins, right there in my first year of NHL hockey. That was fine with me because Boston had a strong team; I came from the Boston area and liked the players on the club.

Tiny Thompson was the goaltender. Eddie Shore and Lionel Hitchman were the first-string defensemen with George Owen and myself as second-stringers. Up front we had Harry Oliver, Perk Galbraith, Cooney Weiland, and Dutch Gainor.

Dutch was the only man I ever saw in hockey who had a double shift. He'd come at a man, fake it one way, fake it to the other, and then walk right through.

Shore was the best of all. He was a lot like Ted Williams in that he could help a teammate if you wanted help. Eddie was very fair about things; if you asked him how to play this or that man, he'd tell you. He didn't withhold advice. Personally, I liked Shore. He was the greatest hockey player I ever saw. He could skate like Bobby Orr and he could shoot. And he was a great defenseman who could hit. He was a dynamic person who could really lift a team.

One night we took off for a game in Montreal; it was a wintry night, snowing and all that. What happens? Shore misses the train. The rest of the club was rolling up to Montreal, snug on the train, while Shore got a hold of a Cadillac from a friend of his and drove all night through the mountains in blizzards and then into the next day and arrived in Montreal about an hour before the game. He got into a uniform and we beat the Canadiens 2–1. Shore scored both goals.

I know some people have said Shore was a vicious player but I don't believe they saw him play too much. Let's say he was a tough, rough player who could give it out as well as take it without complaining.

Having players like Shore and Hitchman on defense meant that I didn't play all that much since they kept the stars out there most of the time—and rightly so; after all it was a money game.

Needless to say, my own personal schedule was different from the other players' since I was going to law school. On Monday the team would practice from noon to 1:00 PM and I'd practice with them after coming from morning classes. Then I'd go back to school in the afternoon.

Tuesday night was game night in Boston and I wouldn't have any practice that day. I'd study all day long and at 6:00 in the evening I'd have my dinner; then at 7:30 I'd go down to the Garden, only a few blocks away, dress, and play the game.

On Wednesday, there'd be a 12:00-to-1:00 PM practice or maybe 1:00-to-2:00 PM and the same on Thursday. Occasionally we'd play in New York on Thursdays and the team would leave in the morning while I was at school and I'd take the noon or 1:00 PM train. I'd study all the way down to New York, get off and go to Madison Square Garden, play the game, and come back with the team on the midnight train and get into Boston in the early morning, then go to classes.

We always had games on weekends so I'd usually catch the 9:00 train on Fridays for Montreal, Ottawa, or Toronto, depending on where we happened to be playing that Saturday night. Wherever we were, I'd stay in the hotel all day with the books then go to the game at night and take the 9:00 again back to Boston on Sunday morning.

Every so often there was a conflict between my hockey schedule and law school. Once we had a game in Detroit when I was supposed to be taking my midyear exams. The solution was supplied by the law school, which let me take my exams at the University of Detroit. They sent the exam out ahead, and when the team departed for the next game in Chicago, I was left behind in Detroit. I took the exam on a Friday and Detroit University sent the papers back to Boston while I got the train to Chicago. They were very cooperative that way.

From time to time people would ask me whether it was difficult concentrating on the books. Actually, playing was an incentive, and I was doing quite well in the NHL. We knocked off the Canadiens in the first round of the Stanley Cup playoffs, then took the Rangers to win the Cup. I wound up getting that full share of the playoff cut I had demanded of Lester Patrick. But then I had an unfortunate accident that affected my hockey career.

During the summer after my rookie season in the NHL I was playing baseball on Cape Cod. One day a bunch of us were in a car, driving to a game, when the car was forced off the road. I came out of the accident with a broken bone in my knee and three fractured vertebrae in my spine. That kept me out of hockey for a whole year and I could never again skate as fast as I did before the accident.

To compensate for the loss of speed I began concentrating more on my defensive play than on rushing with the puck. During my year out of action a few good things happened to me. I was still going to law school and doing well there and at the same time was coaching football at Harvard.

Meanwhile, I had a good chance to study the Bruins as a team and to think about hockey in general. Art Ross was running the Boston club at the time and he was a really tough one, although I had no complaints with him. He was a strict taskmaster but a good hockey man. In those days the club was known as "The Bruising Bruins" and I think the reputation they had as a rough, tough hockey team stemmed from Ross. They hit and hit hard; that's just the way he wanted it.

I realized that I had also learned some of that in New York. In fact, I think Lester Patrick always figured I could stay back to play a little more defense and do a little less rushing. Maybe I did rush too much and perhaps that's why Lester wanted to send me to Springfield. Looking back I'd say he was right, but when a guy comes out of college as I did—a star—he thinks he knows a great deal even though he really doesn't know that much. You don't know real hockey until you get into the pro ranks.

I played against a lot of good men but I think the finest line of all was the one the Rangers had with Frank Boucher centering Bill and Bun Cook. I haven't seen their equal yet. They played together so much and knew each other's moves so perfectly that watching them move the puck around was like observing how a clock works.

Today the players skate much faster and push the puck a lot but there isn't the clever stick work we had in my time. Now it's a game of shove and push,

Lane went on to play defense for the Rangers and the Boston Bruins before becoming a New York State Supreme Court Justice. (Dartmouth Athletic Communications)

hoping to score with blind shots. I think possibly half the goals scored today are because the goalie is screened and doesn't see the puck.

Nels Stewart was another great. He was slow but deadly with the stick and tremendous around the net. Aurel Joliat of the Canadiens was another terrific stickhandler. He must have weighed about 118 pounds soaking wet but he was a wizard at handling the puck. He had a funny habit of always wearing a black baseball cap when he played and word around the league was that if you knocked Joliat's black cap off his head he'd get so mad it'd hurt his play. Well, naturally the Bruins would try to knock that cap off and it certainly did upset him. Joliat played on a line with Howie Morenz and Johnny Gagnon and they were quite a bunch.

Howie Morenz was the fastest thing I ever saw on ice. He'd be in full speed after taking only two strides. Offhand, I'd say he was one of the greatest hockey players of all time. Being on the shelf that one year I really had a good chance to see them all. I'm sure Ross knew I'd eventually quit hockey to go into law. But that didn't matter to him and he did get some work out of me the year I was out with the injury.

Those were the days when the Bruins had a farm club called the Boston Cubs. They were a good minor league team in need of a manager so Ross put me in charge; it turned out to be a very rewarding experience. When I took over they were in last place and by the season's end we were on top.

The Cubs consisted of a bunch of young fellows going up to the NHL and a group of veterans who had come down. There was a fellow on the team named Joe Giroux who was a little firecracker and nobody could handle him, not even Ross. Here I was, the collegian with a broken back, running this club, trying to control Giroux, and attempting to bring them up from last place.

For some reason I was determined to work with Giroux and help him, even though everybody else had dropped him because he was so wild. I knew he was a great hockey player; all he needed was a little balance. Well, I hadn't been with the Cubs too long when Joe came to me with a problem.

He said, "You know those penalties I get for sometimes losing my head? Well, I don't mind them so much but the $25 fine is cutting into my income. How can I stay on the ice without getting fined?"

I began thinking to myself, *How am I going to keep him in the game?* I started playing for time and finally inquired, "Joe why are you asking me that question?"

He replied, "Myles, you're going to law school. You know all the answers!"

I said I wished I did but knew I had to give him some advice, so I said, "Well, Joe, I'll tell you what you have to do. The next time anybody whacks you out on that ice, count to 10 before you do anything else."

Joe looked at me and said, "Why 10?"

"Because," I told him, "one of two things will happen. Number one: if the man you hit hasn't broken a leg, he'll skate out of reach, so should you swing that stick at him you'll miss him. Number two: at the end of the count you'll be all over your mad, so you'll stay on the ice. Right?"

"Well, I'll try it," he said, and for the next month he was the star of the league. Then it happened.

We went to play a game against New Haven at their rink and they had a Polish fellow on their team by the name of Dutkowski. As the game moved along I could see Joe's temper was rising because Dutkowski was bothering him. With only eight or 10 minutes left, we were leading by one goal, however, and I was hopeful everything would be all right.

Dutkowski, a former Chicago Black Hawk, skated near Joe and suddenly Joe hit him over the head with his stick with such a clout that it looked as if a geyser of blood was coming out of Dutkowski's head. They carried him off the ice and there was almost a riot. A special platoon of police was called in and Joe was put off with a match penalty. Then New Haven scored two goals and beat us.

Later that night we were on the train back to Boston and I was sitting and fuming about the incident when in comes Joe, acting like a big St. Bernard. He just sat there watching me and finally asked, "Myles, what's the trouble?"

"Are you kidding?" I said. "Look, Joe, I've been treating you like a brother. I figured to send you back to the major leagues. I've built you up all year long; that's all right, it's part of my job. But you came to me, wanting to know all about my law experience. You asked me how to stay on the ice—and what do you do, Joe? You disgraced me out there."

"Disgrace you! How?" he said.

"You went out there," I said, "and hit some guy over the head, fractured his skull, and we lost the game. I feel like you've let me down."

He said, "Myles, I didn't let you down."

"Joe," I asked, "what did I tell you to do?"

"You told me to count to 10, didn't you?" he said.

I said, "Yes."

"And you said I could swing my stick," he told me; I agreed but added, "You didn't count to 10."

"Yes, I did," he insisted.

I said, "Joe, look, when you got into that bumping with Dutkowski, I started to count and got to five and then you let that stick go."

He replied, "Myles, I forgot to tell you one thing. You know I was born in Poland and came over to Canada when I was seven or eight years old. Whenever I get mad I forget to count in English, so I do it in Polish and count twice as fast. When I was bumping Dutkowski I counted to 10 in Polish, let the stick go, and he was in the way!"

What could I say to that?

We had a good team and after my year of recuperation I was ready to return to the NHL. One night I'll never forget was the Eddie Shore–Ace Bailey incident.

We were playing Toronto at Boston Garden and the local papers had more or less played up the game as a grudge match. As far as Ace was concerned, though, he was one of the nicest men ever to play hockey. On this night Shore had rushed down the length of the ice and Red Horner of Toronto, no shrinking violet himself, pushed Shore into the boards and really hit him hard. Shore struck his head and down he went.

Horner got the puck and went up the ice while Bailey dropped back on the Toronto defense. To this day I really believe Shore was so dizzy getting up that he thought the man in front of him was Horner, not Bailey.

As he went by Ace, Shore just dragged his stick. He didn't bump Ace; he just took the skates out from under him. Not expecting it, Ace fell backward and struck his head on the ice and suddenly he started to shudder.

Meanwhile, Shore skated back and stood there on defense, dazed. Horner skated up to him, took his gloves off, wound up like a pitcher would before throwing a fastball, and hit Shore on the chin. Shore fell backward, hitting his head on the ice.

Bailey was taken into the Toronto dressing room normally used by the Cubs. The Cubs trainer, Joe Gilmore, had enough presence of mind to get chopped ice to encase Bailey's head. He looked like a mummy but I think the ice saved his life; he was bleeding inside and that ice kept the bleeding down. He had a double fracture of the skull, one on each side.

In the Bruins dressing room they took 18 stitches in Shore's head and he was out, although few people knew that. Bailey was rushed to the hospital where Dr. Munro, a famous brain surgeon, operated on him. They put two silver plates in his head. Of course, we didn't know what would happen to him but we still had the schedule to fulfill and went to New York for a game two nights later.

Shore was suspended for the rest of the year, and as far as the Bruins were concerned, they might as well have quit—they were finished. They couldn't play anymore, but they had to. I remember that night in New York; we were getting regular reports on Bailey's condition, which was quite serious. They didn't think he was going to live and he remained on the danger list for quite a while. Ace eventually recovered but never played hockey again. Shore came back a season later and was still a great player.

As for me, I finally finished my law studies and quit hockey. I wanted to come to New York so I said, "Good-bye, NHL, you've helped me a lot. I'm never going to be a star; I've got a broken back. Thanks again for everything."

I got a job with President Roosevelt's old law firm, Roosevelt and O'Connor, and went to the U.S. Attorney's office as an assistant. During World War II, I spent four years in the Navy, then back to civilian life with a job as chief assistant at the U.S. Attorney's office. I became U.S. Attorney and after that was chairman of the New York State Crime Commission for 10 years and a partner in the firm of Schwartz and Froelich. Then I was elected to the New York State Supreme Court.

I still enjoy hockey but think the game could be improved a bit. The one thing I don't see enough of is the real bodychecking or the stickhandling we used to have. I feel it's important to keep the speed in the game and am a firm believer in the importance of the forward pass.

There could be some changes made in the defensive zone—allowing only lateral passing there offensively. That might bring back the old-time body-checking and more stickhandling. I'd allow forward passing from the net right up to the red line, but only lateral passing to the second blue line and in the defensive zone.

Today, if a defensive man tries to hit an opponent at his blue line it takes one man out of the play because the offensive player passes up to someone ahead of him. Because they allow that forward passing in the defensive zone there's more emphasis on stickchecking than bodychecking. If a man tries to throw a bodycheck he winds up out of the play.

Crowds want three things today: scoring, which there is; good stickhandling, which there isn't; and speed, which there certainly is.

But professional hockey has changed since I played; it's now a money game, not a sport, a sales job that consists of giving the public what it wants. Today, hockey is getting the crowds but if attendance ever drops off the owners will have to put in more hitting and stickwork—and that's when I'll enjoy the game again.

chapter three

Tom Lockhart

Rangers Business Manager and the Busiest Executive in Hockey

BORN: New York, New York, March 21, 1892

DIED: May 18, 1979

POSITION: Business Manager, New York Rangers, 1947–53

AWARDS/HONORS: Hockey Hall of Fame, 1965

Among all Rangers executives over the years, none had a more complex and fascinating hockey life than Tom Lockhart.

At one point, the native New Yorker not only was business manager of the Blueshirts but also was the business manager of the New Haven Ramblers of the American League, manager of the New York Rovers of the Eastern Amateur League, president of the Eastern Amateur League, and president of the Amateur Hockey Association of the United States.

Lockhart entered the hockey picture in 1932 when he was called in to reorganize amateur hockey in Madison Square Garden. After that he became the key man in organized amateur hockey in the United States, responsible for more boys in the States taking up the game than anyone else.

Ironically Tom never played hockey, although he gained fame as a track man and a bike rider. When his competitive days were at an end, he stepped into the administrative end of athletics, as a member of the managing board of the Amateur

Athletic Union's Metropolitan Association. It was while he was in charge of that organization's amateur boxing that Tom was approached to enter the hockey field.

By 1947 when Lockhart took over the role of Rangers business manager he and Frank Boucher had succeeded Lester Patrick in command of the Rangers.

Tom was the first executive of a National Hockey League team—other than president or vice president—who was born in the United States. Add to this distinction the fact that Thomas F. Lockhart was without a doubt the busiest hockey executive of all time, regardless of place of birth.

I met Lockhart for the first time when I was in the Rangers Fan Club. I suggested to him that I could help promote hockey by writing a newsletter about the Eastern League. Tommy obliged me and in a sense became one of my early mentors. Nearly two decades later I sat with him at his Upper East Side Manhattan apartment along with his daughter, Madeline.

It was December 1971 and Tommy was in A-1 form, recalling stories from his colorful past.

Our oral history begins with Lockhart detailing how a nonhockey man such as himself wound up being the busiest executive in the ice game.

Before I was asked to take a job in hockey I was actually running the boxing shows in the old Madison Square Garden on Eighth Avenue and 50th Street. That was right around the corner from where I was born so you can't consider me a hockey man like those Canadians. I'm New York all the way. My father was born on 27th Street in Manhattan, so that makes me an original Indian. In fact, I'm waiting to get it back from them for $36.

I remember meeting Teddy Roosevelt as a kid. My dad took me down to the police headquarters and I shook the great man's hand. He told me about the time he rode up one hill and down the other in the Spanish-American War. Roosevelt was police commissioner when I met him.

Hockey wasn't even on my mind in those days. I got into sports as a bicycle rider in competition, then did some track and field running for the St. John's Club on 56th Street. Out of that I somehow became their representative to the Amateur Athletic Union. Then I got into the boxing end of it and eventually wound up running the matches at the Garden.

Then the damnedest thing happened: I became involved with hockey because the bosses at the Garden wanted me to throw it out. In those days—the early 1930s—they had Sunday afternoon amateur hockey, as well as the Rangers' and Americans' pro games, and the afternoon games weren't doing any business.

The Garden management had just brought in General John Reed Kilpatrick to get rid of things in the building that weren't paying off and he called me in with some other AAU officers to eliminate the Sunday afternoon hockey. That didn't hit me right so I told the General he was making a big mistake; I figured amateur hockey could make a go of it if it was run right.

"Look," the General said, "I'll go along and give Sunday hockey another try, under one condition: it has to be run by one man, not the way it is now with a big committee."

One of the guys at the meeting was Fred Rubien, chairman of the National AAU. He went in to talk privately with the General after the meeting was over and nothing had been decided. Meantime, I went back to the Garden, and about 5:00 PM Rubin came back and walked over to me to say, "The General told me he knows somebody who should take the hockey job; he's talking about you."

I said, "What'd I do now? What the hell do I know about hockey?" We stood there talking for about 20 minutes when who walks out of the elevator but the General himself. He says, "Tommy, come up and see me at 10:00 tomorrow morning." I did and he told me he wanted me to take the hockey job, alone. And that was that. Me, Tommy Lockhart, who had never even owned a pair of roller skates let alone ice skates, had to sell amateur ice hockey at the Garden.

At that time we had three amateur teams playing: St. Nick's, the Crescent Club, and the New York Athletic Club. My idea to promote hockey was the same I had used for boxing: promotions, cut-rate tickets, and contacts. I had several contacts in the AAU that served as a starter but we needed a break and got it in a strange way that connected Mayor Jimmy Walker and Dan Parker, sports editor for the old *Mirror*.

A sportsman fellow named Blumenthal decided the winning team should get a trophy in honor of Jimmy Walker so he went to Cartier's and bought one for $500; it became the Walker Cup. Somehow, after the Cup was first presented, it wound up in a hock shop on Eighth Avenue and I was tipped off about it and went up to the General with the story. Dan Parker wrote it up in

Tom Lockhart (seated, middle) was a key member of the Rangers front office in the 1950s and was inducted into the Hockey Hall of Fame in 1965. (U.S. Hockey Hall of Fame Museum)

the *Mirror*: Jimmy Walker was in exile in Mexico and his Cup was exiled in a hock shop on Eighth Avenue. "What do you want to do about it?" I asked the General. "Bail it out!" he said. So I went down and got the hockey cup for $80.

Parker did us a big favor by giving us a whole column about the Walker Cup and also about Sunday afternoon hockey. He had been coming every Sunday to the games with his grandchild and he loved it. That started the people coming with their kids but we still needed more than that. We got another break that summer when some other promoters decided to organize a hockey league up and down the East Coast.

I got wind they were having the meeting on the Fourth of July at the Penn Athletic Club in Philadelphia and decided to invite a friend who was also connected with hockey. I was supposed to meet him at Penn Station; he showed up with a girl and by the time we reached Philadelphia they were both so drunk I had to get porters to take them off the train.

When I finally arrived at the Athletic Club, the guy at the desk told me the hockey meeting was all over. "They must've gone home," he said. "But take a look, just in case."

I walked into the room and, sure enough, some people were sitting around the table and one of them asked what I was doing there. I replied, "I came down here to join the league." What else could I say? They then said, "Look, we're making the schedule. We're all set to go."

At that point John Carlin, a real Yankee Doodle Boy, jumped up and pointed at me, "Did you say you wanted to put a team in this league?" I replied, "Yes sir."

He asked how many and I said, "three teams." Then he wanted to know where, and when I answered Madison Square Garden, he said, "You're in!" The others protested, "But he can't be." Carlin said, "Tear up that schedule. What the hell's the matter with you guys!" You see, they needed the Garden and I had it—so they needed me.

After much discussion they concluded, "Well, if he's coming in, he's going to have to make up the schedule." We finally decided to keep the first two weeks the way they had it and then I'd take it from there. The next item was to pick the name of the new league.

Until that time somebody'd been using a rubber stamp for the papers with the same "Eastern Amateur Lacrosse League" on it and I had the thing in my pocket. I took it out, looked at it, and said, "Somebody take the Lacrosse out and put in Hockey." And that's exactly how the Eastern Amateur Hockey League got its name. I don't know who wound up with the rubber stamp.

That first season we had seven teams: Baltimore, Atlantic City, Hershey, the Bronx, St. Nick's, New York A.C., and the Crescents. When I got back to the Garden the next day I went over to see Jack Filman, who was doing the broadcasting from the Garden's own radio station. He busted the story and soon everybody was talking about Eastern Amateur Hockey League. But my problems were just beginning. They had decided to go with a 48-game-schedule—24 home games, 24 away—which put me in a hole since I had only 16 Sunday afternoon dates at the Garden. One of the first things I did was to make deals with each of the clubs to play my home games in their rinks for $250 and the cost of getting down there and back.

It worked out well. Those fellows would get gates they'd never had before and it all helped to encourage interest in hockey and the league. My problems still weren't over. I couldn't accommodate all of the extra games so I had to cheat a little. I'd make up phony games; have the Crescents beating the New York A.C. 1–0 and put down somebody's name for scoring the goal and add an assist or two. Then the next week I'd add two more and a couple of ties. Turned out 21 games were never played but nobody noticed it—at least no one in the league.

One time a fellow from the *Times* got interested in the league and started asking questions about these games. I said, "Well, I'll tell you. You know the Rangers play on Tuesday nights. The Americans play on Thursday night, and the next week it's the reverse. I'd have the teams in there playing in the afternoons. We call them 'dark house' games. The seats were standing up and cheering." But it actually happened—21 games never occurred and the league finished its full schedule of games played in that first year.

By the time the season was over we were selling out the Garden. Our trick was a little different from today's procedures. As you left the building after seeing a game you could buy your ticket for next week—before they went on general sale. That meant we almost sold out a week in advance.

By the middle of the summer we began getting letters about tickets for the new schedule. We struck it good because we were catering to the little fellow, the working man. The first year we sold tickets at 25 cents for any seat in the house. Then it went up to 50 and 75 cents but that wasn't bad because the little fellow knew that every Sunday if he had 75 cents or half a dollar he'd have the same seat as when he bought his first ticket. A man could bring three kids for less than $3. The father was happy and so were the kids. They saw a game or they could run all over the place; we didn't chase kids like they do today.

Another thing people liked was our program. It had no ads, just all kinds of columns—a gossip column, a league column—in short, plenty of reading material. We used to sell more programs in one day than the Rangers would in two games. And nobody left their program in the building; there was so much in it to take home and read. That was all part of my principle: you give them something they have to take home and when a friend comes into the house, sees it, and asks what that's all about, the fan tells him and we have another customer.

All the fuss over the Sunday afternoon amateur hockey ultimately seeped down to the Rangers office and pretty soon I got a call from manager Lester Patrick. He thought we had a good thing going and felt he could help.

I said, "Great, what can you do?"

"Well," he offered, "next season I could bring you some good hockey players in from Canada." One word led to another and we decided to ice only one team instead of the three and spent half a day trying to name it. We had the Rangers and the Ramblers so we "roved" between and called it the Rovers.

Before our season began Lester went up to Winnipeg for the start of his training camp and picked out some good young players for us. We eventually wound up with Mac and Neil Colville, Alex Shibicky, Murray Patrick, Joe Cooper, and Bert Gardiner—two defensemen, three forwards, and a goaltender. We started with about 10 men and never had more than 11 and we played and won the league championship with 11.

The trouble with hockey now is that they have too many men. They sit on the bench too long and don't get ice. That way they don't develop the way they used to when we had the Eastern League. And we also had a lot more interesting things for the customers. A lot more.

I used to have figure skaters come in and skate between periods. Did you know I was the one to bring Shipstad and Johnson [a touring ice show] into the Garden for the first time? They had come off the outdoor rinks in Minnesota, then played the Colony Club in Chicago. We saw their act and booked them into the Garden even though they had never skated on arena ice before. Well, that was something. There was a big difference between our Garden ice and the nightclub stuff. Maybe that's what made them.

I'll never forget their first appearance. It was between periods of our hockey game and Shipstad and Johnson were in the dressing room, very nervous.

Then they got the call to go out and they ran for the entrance, both at once. The second they hit the ice both of them fell right on their behinds—the house went bananas. They got up, did their act, and came off moaning, "Well, I guess we're finished as an act."

A minute later one of the Garden big shots walks into their dressing room to say, "That was a helluva act!" "What?" they say. And he says, "The next time you go out there, do it again." The boys ask, "Do what?" And he says, "Fall!" That fall put the Shipstad and Johnson show on the road and led to their Ice Follies. Made a fortune for them both.

That wasn't all; we also gave Sonja Henie her debut. She had just won the Olympics and was coming to New York for a visit, so the General contacted me to say she was turning pro and that we should get her to skate at the Garden.

We had a Rovers game scheduled in the afternoon and an All-Star event in the evening so we figured we'd put Sonja on in between. Some Swedish organization was in charge of selling tickets and they sold the place out, but everyone had to come to the Rovers game first since they didn't know exactly when she'd go on.

What a sight. A terrific game was going on but for 30 odd minutes you could've heard a pin drop. Nobody made a sound whether the guys scored or not. Nothing. At the end of the period the teams went back to their dressing rooms completely disgusted. They had played fantastically but nobody reacted.

Then Sonja came out and the roof fell in. Everyone in the stands was Swedish, you see. It was some show and we decided to have Sonja skate everywhere we had an Eastern League game. Hershey, Baltimore, Atlantic City—and the Rovers were the supporting cast. Still, she was a funny duck and never my cup of tea.

No doubt about it, Sonja Henie was a tough act to follow but we managed to top her with a live bear and, believe it or not, we even flew airplanes in the Garden. Whenever somebody came in with a suggestion I'd try it. If you said you wanted to come to the hockey game and walk the length of the ice on your head, Tom Lockhart would bill you. The airplanes were an example.

When I tell you we flew airplanes in the Garden I'm not kidding. It started with this big toymaker in the city. He walked into the Garden one afternoon with an idea: airplane races. He was putting out toy airplanes—the ones we had as kids that you'd run with and they'd go up in the air, their wheels turning—and he wanted us to race them on the ice. So we took a couple of the players in the Metropolitan League, lined them up at one end of the rink before the Rovers game, and had them skate three or four laps around the Garden and then pick a winner. That's how we flew airplanes in the building.

Another guy wanted to have bicycle races on the ice. Since I was an experienced bike-racer I knew it wouldn't be easy to make those turns and told the guy, "I'll prove you can't." I got on the bike and pedaled up a head of steam but when I got near the endboards I damn near killed myself. I told him if the frame could be altered it might work, but I'm glad we dropped the idea because we might have killed somebody. Working with live bears was a lot easier, believe me.

The bear was Jack Filman's idea. He was doing publicity for the Garden at the rink and told me he'd seen this great act at a roller skating rink. I asked what the act was like and he replied, "There's a bear that skates." I said, "How can he skate? And if he does, he's skating on a roller floor." Filman said, "Well, we can put him on ice skates, couldn't we?"

One discussion led to another and we decided that maybe we could do something with it. So we went up to take a look at the bear. The bear's owner was a foreigner and it must have taken eight hours for us to explain to him what we were trying to do and for him to say what his bear could do. He'd tell me the bear roller skates and I'd tell him I'm not interested in roller skates, I want him to ice skate. If we'd say skates he would say he's got skates. Finally, he got the message.

We then asked how much he wanted, but before he could answer I said, "I'll give you $20," and he agreed.

With that settled the next trick was to get the bear into the Garden before our Sunday afternoon doubleheader. I didn't want anybody at the Garden to know there was a bear coming in because there'd be hell to pay if they heard about it. It might start a ruckus and there'd be 18 guys wanting to know who's going to hold the bear.

After a while I figured out the best technique. Early that Sunday morning I went down to the employees' entrance on 49th Street and talked to the guy at the door. I said, "There's a cab coming here with Jack Filman and a bear."

He says, "Wha'?"

I said, "I want you to let him in. Open Room 29 and get the bear in there. And don't talk about it!"

Sure enough, Filman brings the bear, we lock him in Room 29, and then he and I put our heads together because we've got a big problem: where are we going to get skates for the bear? I mean now we're dealing with a size 40 shoe. We went to the Rangers equipment room and the biggest skate we could find would only go as far as the bear's instep. Meantime, Harry Westerby, the Rangers trainer, is screaming at us for taking his equipment for a bear. After we explained the act to him he suddenly got enthusiastic and finally came up with the longest skate on the hockey team.

The next question was how to put the skates on the bear. By then it was past noon and everybody in the back of the Garden was getting into the act. The Met League game was starting and people were in the building, so we had to be sure the cops didn't let anybody through to the back to disturb the bear. We had decided to attach the skates to the bear's feet with rope, which we did, making it pretty secure.

All of a sudden the bear's owner chimes in that the bear can't go skating on the ice unless *he* goes out with him, and he's got to have skates, too. The search is on again; we find skates, put them on the foreigner, and then learn he's never been on ice skates in his life. He's even having trouble standing up in one place just in the room. While all this is going on the bear is using the room as a toilet and the cleanup crew had to come in with a pail and mop several times. It got so bad that the next day the Sanitation Department had to come in and disinfect the room.

Anyway, once we got a cord for the trainer to attach to the bear we were about ready. I said, "Wait a minute, we ought to tell the two teams what we're up to." It was the Rovers against the Hershey Bears. I mentioned that the bear will come out and the trainer would be with him on skates, even though he couldn't skate. We had the thing perfectly timed out and the electricians had the spotlights ready. I made the countdown: "Four, three, two, one!"

We bring the bear out, with the guy holding the cord. He lets five feet, then 10 feet out…and falls flat on his stomach. But he wouldn't let go of that cord; he just hung on as the bear skated all over the ice pulling him around the rink.

By this time the people were up on their seats. I looked around and saw the General sitting there and enjoying it; everybody was having a great time. They were all howling but now I knew we had another problem: how were we going to get the bear *off* the ice? That big fella was just skating all over the place with no intentions of leaving and we had a hockey game to play. Already I had all kinds of advisors since the whole back-of-the-Garden crowd was in on this, but nobody could do a thing that worked. Finally, some woman walked up to me right out of the blue and said, "You want the bear off the ice?" I replied, "Yeah, of course I want the bear off the ice!"

Next thing I know she walks out onto the ice, no skates, no nothin', puts her two fingers into her mouth, whistles, and sure enough the bear comes over, pulling the Italian guy behind him like a car pulling a trailer. We took the bear back to his dressing room and along comes the General who said he thought we had a helluva act. It was so good we took it down to Hershey and it was a hit there, too.

Boy, did we have fun in those days. I can tell you a good one about when I once told a group of intelligent people how ice hockey started. The first time I told this story was in the 23rd Street YMCA in the late 1930s. That was when Murray Patrick, Lester's big son, was playing for the Rangers.

One day Murray walked into my office and said, "My father wants me to go down and play in New Haven." So I answered, "Well, what the hell do you want me to do, argue with your father?" He said, "No, no, that ain't it. There's a friend of mine down at the Y and I promised to go there Saturday night and talk about ice hockey; I also sent a film down."

I told Murray not to worry about it; I'd get one of the Met League guys to go to the Y instead. But I forgot all about it until that Saturday night when a friend of mine from the Met League, Al Such, walked in. I said, "Hey, what're you doin' tonight? I'll buy you a dinner and we'll go down to the Y and give a hockey talk."

We arrived and they showed the film. When it was over a fellow came on stage and announced, "Tonight, we have one of the greatest hockey players in the world to tell you about ice hockey: Mr. Tom Lockhart!" With that I scrambled up on the stage and got a hand.

"I'll tell you my experience in playing ice hockey," I began. "As a kid I lived on the East Side and in the winter we'd go up to Central Park. I went there one day with a pair of skates and sat down by the side of the lake and tied the skates on. Finally, I stood up and wet my pants! That's my experience with ice hockey." When they heard that they whistled and cheered like mad.

You never knew what you were going to come up with in that Eastern League. I remember the time a dirt farmer from River Vale, New Jersey, got the bug to get in hockey and had an arena built out there in the sticks—at least it was the sticks then—and Lester Patrick and I went out to see the guy.

We got him into the league the following year and in a strange sort of way he was responsible for making Bill Chadwick the great referee he turned out to be later on. I already had Chadwick working in the Eastern League and one night he refereed in River Vale. The next day he came into my office to say he's quitting.

"I ain't never goin' back to River Vale," he fumed. "This guy, [John] Handwerg, abused me too much."

That infuriated me. I told him, "You get back there next Sunday with your skates." He did and I took him to the dressing room and we walked right past Handwerg without a peep. After Chadwick put his skates on I said, "Bill, when you go out on the ice I'll be sitting there right by the bench and I'll be at this gate when you come off. In other words I'll be backing you all the way."

And that's exactly what happened. The game was over and Bill and I went back to the referee's room. After about a minute there was a rap at the door; it was Handwerg. He asked if he could come in and then walked over to Chadwick and said, "I'm sorry, Bill. I'll never abuse you again."

To me, that was the turning point in Chadwick's career. Bill then went on to become one of the best referees in NHL history. But he wasn't the only good one we had. There was a little ref called Mickey Slowik who nearly got killed by a player named Joe Desson; this was in a playoff game in New Haven against Johnstown. Desson was a big defenseman with New Haven and at one point Slowik blew his whistle and pointed his finger at Desson to go to the penalty box. Slowik then turned to the penalty timekeeper along the boards to give him the details of the penalty.

But Mickey had made the mistake of not waiting for Desson to go to the penalty box. Suddenly Desson came up behind with his stick, banged Slowik

Lockhart began his long association with hockey in 1932 when he was asked to organize amateur hockey at Madison Square Garden. (U.S. Hockey Hall of Fame Museum)

pretty hard, and knocked him clear into the stands. All hell broke loose. Finally, a cop stepped right out onto the ice, arrested Desson, and another cop came and they took him to court for inciting a riot. Everybody wondered what I would do as president of the league. I suspended him for life.

A lot of people were really against Joe, but to me, he was all right. It's all in how you look at things; some people whisper, some people shout. You look for trouble when you think a guy is going to give it to you but the principle is that everybody in his own environment is a king and dies just like I do. So there's no difference. Desson was a hard player but he wasn't alone. I saw some dillies in my day, and I can remember one time when the craziest thing happened to a quiet guy—Art Coulter—who played defense for Lester on the Rangers.

Lester and I were sitting together in the seats next to the penalty box when Coulter got a penalty; I don't recall what it was for but I do know Lester was wearing a new hat and was very proud of it. So Coulter, known for being a very reserved guy with not much of a temper, came into the box, about to sit down, and what do you think happens? He goes berserk. First, he grabbed Lester's new hat and started beating me over the head with it. Lester's yelling, "Gimme my hat back!" and I'm covering my head wondering what I ever did to deserve that beating. This took all of five or 10 seconds and then just as quickly as it started, it ended. Coulter sat down, Lester grabbed his hat, I straightened it out, and everything returned to normal.

Like I said, lots of interesting things happened. When I was running the Eastern League in the mid-1940s we worked out a deal one year where we played teams from the Quebec Senior League: Montreal, Sherbrooke, Shawinigan Falls, Quebec City, and Valleyfield. Not too many people remember but I was the one who had the first all-black line playing at Madison Square Garden when we had the tie-up with the Quebec League. The line played for Sherbrooke and was composed of the Carnegie Brothers, Herbie and Ossie, and Manny McIntyre—they were terrific. Then I had a Chinese player, Larry Kwong, on the Rovers for quite a while and several other characters. Hank D'Amore was one, and now there's a story for you.

During World War II, I was sitting in my office one day when this short, chubby fellow walked in. Bear in mind that many of the players were in the Army then and it was very hard to get enough men to fill out a team. This guy looked just like the comedian Lou Costello from Abbott and Costello and he says, "I want to play hockey for you."

"Sure," I answered, "I'll give you $10 a week and you're on." Naturally, I was kidding about the pay but in the same breath he comes back and replies, "I'll take it!"

By now I wondered what I was getting into so I told him I'd better see what he could do on the ice. He went to the dressing room, got fitted out, and then attended a Rovers practice. It turns out he not only can skate and shoot but he's one of the best men on the ice, if not *the* best. "C'mon down to my office," I told him.

D'Amore changed into his regular clothes and walked in. "Well," he asked, "was I all right? Can I play for you?"

"You not only can play for me," I answered, "but I'm going to make you coach!" And I meant it. At that time we also had a team called the Crescents from the old Brooklyn Ice Palace, so I made D'Amore the playing coach and gave him a heck of a lot more money than he ever bargained for. Later we switched him over to the Rovers and he became one of the most popular players we ever had.

In addition to the Rovers, we also were running the Met League, which was composed of players both young and old from the New York area. Chadwick came up from that league and so did a lot of other good ones. Dom Baolto, later an NHL linesman, Mike Nardello, Mickey Slowik—they were just a few.

The Met Leaguers would play their game of three 15-minute periods at 1:30 PM and then the Rovers would come on at 3:30 on Sunday afternoons. The Rovers had the usual 20-minute periods, but even though the Met Leaguers weren't as good they played exciting hockey and the fans loved them. One night they managed to save the Rangers a great deal of embarrassment.

It was in the 1950s and we were having our usual Sunday doubleheader; the Met Leaguers had finished and the Rovers game was on. That night the Rangers were supposed to play the Red Wings but both teams were coming in from out of town and there had been a fierce blizzard all up and down the Eastern Seaboard. We were in the first period of the Rovers game when a phone call came in from Lynn Patrick, then the Rangers coach. "We're stuck in Buffalo," he tells me, "and there's no way we can get to New York in time for the game." He said they'd probably make it to the Garden eventually but he had no idea when the train would be able to pull out of Buffalo.

The Garden was in big trouble. They'd have 15,000 people in the building for the night game and no teams to play hockey and I was the guy who they asked to save the whole shebang for them. Well, I got on the phone and called all the Met League coaches—Harold Heinz, Al Such, the whole bunch—and told them to get their players and be at the Garden promptly at 7:30 PM.

In those days Rangers games started at 8:30 so we had a little time to prepare. The question was whether we'd be able to scrape up enough of them to make a game of it since many of the kids had already gone home after playing their game and we didn't know where they'd be by now.

By 7:00 that night I couldn't believe it—a swamp of them showed up, enough for two full teams. We called them the Met League All-Stars and promptly at 8:30 put two teams on the ice. Everybody in the place was skeptical, including me, but then some magic happened. Those Met Leaguers played like they never did before; they must've thought they were in the NHL the way they went at it, and soon the entire crowd was roaring as though it was a Stanley Cup Finals. They played two periods of the greatest hockey anybody ever saw. The only thing that annoyed the people was that we were about to start the third period when the Rangers and Red Wings showed up and we couldn't finish the game.

The Met Leaguers were a tough act to follow but the Rangers came through that night, too. They put on a terrific show against an equally great Detroit team that ended early in the morning. Everybody went home happy.

That Met League exhibition proved something to me: an American kid can play the game as well as any Canadian youngster as long as the American has enough ice. In those days our trouble was that you couldn't find enough places where the kids could play. In the whole city of New York maybe a handful of rinks existed. That really burned Lester Patrick because he wanted an American player on the Rangers in the worst way.

Incidents like the night the Met Leaguers wowed the Rangers fans are good for hockey; they create a new interest. People who had never read about hockey were suddenly hearing about the American kids. These are the stories. The normal game stuff is nothing—it's the same every week. So when you get a situation like that or have a bear skate at the Garden or hold airplane races, you get people saying, "Gee, they've got quite an act. You've never seen anything like it." That's fun, and it was good for hockey.

chapter four

Gerry Cosby
Rangers Backup Goalie and Equipment King

BORN: Roxbury, Massachusetts, May 15, 1909

DIED: November 26, 1996

POSITION: Practice Goalie, New York Rangers, 1930s; Boston Bruins, 1930s

AWARDS/HONORS: Gold Medal, 1938 World Ice Hockey Championships; International Ice Hockey Hall of Fame, 1997

Anyone who hung around the Rangers—or their Eastern League's New York Rovers— during the 1930s, 1940s, or 1950s—knew Gerry Cosby. By 1960 his name was a byword in all hockey circles. A New Englander through and through, Cosby starred on the 1933 World Championship Gold Medal–winning team. Cosby had four shut- outs and a 0.108 goals-against average. After that he starred for England's Wembley Lions and also represented Uncle Sam at the 1938 World Championships.

By that time he had come to New York and won a job with the Rangers as their practice goalie while being the netminder for the Rovers, one of the strongest non-NHL teams in North America. Thanks to Rangers czar Lester Patrick, in 1938 Cosby founded the hockey business that would eventually become synony- mous with quality hockey equipment.

I first met Gerry when his store was based in a brownstone living room near Rockefeller Center. My first purchase was a gold hockey tie clip, which I still have to this day.

Eventually Cosby moved his store to the old Madison Square Garden on Eighth Avenue between 49th and 50th streets in Manhattan. When the present MSG opened in 1968, Gerry Cosby Inc. moved to a spot on the 31st Street side of the arena between Seventh and Eighth avenues. By that time Cosby's was operated by Gerry's son Michael.

Four years after the new store opened, I interviewed Gerry. It was January of 1972 and Cosby was 59 years old but still full of vigor and vitality.

We chatted for three hours, and when the clock struck midnight he said he had to leave because the next day he would escort Anatoly Tarasov, the Soviet hockey coach, around his shop.

In our oral history, Cosby picks up with his life immediately preceding his introduction to Lester Patrick and the Rangers.

When I got back to the States I became a runner on Wall Street. That certainly was the toughest job I ever had; when I got home from doing a day's running down there I was ready for bed. I couldn't wait for the start of the next hockey season so I could take a "vacation."

Working on Wall Street put me in New York, so the first thing I did when the fall came was to join the New York Athletic Club because it had a hockey team. Then I decided to go a step further. There were two pro teams in town, the Rangers and the Americans, and I figured they might be able to use a practice goalie.

I called up Lester Patrick, the Rangers coach, and said, "Mr. Patrick, my name is Cosby, Gerry Cosby from Boston. I've been the practice goalie for the Bruins and the Boston Tigers and I'd like to come out and practice with the Rangers."

He replied, "Fine. Come on down, we need somebody. We're practicing tomorrow morning at 11:00."

The next morning I arrived at the old Garden on Eighth Avenue and 49th Street and walked into the dressing room where everybody was standing half-dressed. I figured either Patrick had given me the wrong hour or I had forgotten what time to get there, although I don't think I'd ever forget anything like that. So I went up to Lester and introduced myself.

Well, he saw me standing there, a little guy, a nobody, practically buried by my own equipment, and then he looked around the room at all the major

Rangers practice goalie Gerry Cosby backstopped the United States to a gold medal at the 1938 World Ice Hockey Championships. (Michael Cosby Collection)

leaguers there. They were the best, the cream of hockey stars—Bill and Bun Cook, Frank Boucher, Murray Murdoch, Butch Keeling, and Ching Johnson—and then he turned back to me, and yelled, "Fellows, I want to introduce you to Gerry Cosby. He called me yesterday and he wants to try out for our team!"

I couldn't believe my ears. I had no intention of trying out for the Rangers. All I wanted to do was be the practice goalie as I was in Boston. When I heard Lester say that I felt like going right through the floor. Anyway, he knew what I really meant and let me dress and work out with the club; the next thing I knew I got the job as practice goalie, where I learned plenty.

In 1936, I was notified of my selection as goalie for the United States Olympic team. I'm probably the only player in the history of hockey to turn down an invitation to play in the Olympics but that's what I did, and it was one of the biggest mistakes of my life. I had gotten a job in the construction business with Stewart Iglehart, the great polo player, and at that time business was going well with his firm and he didn't think I should leave just then to play in the Olympics. He was very persuasive and I decided to stay home and continue working for him. The Olympic team was going to carry two goalies, myself and a fellow named Tom Moon from Boston. They ended up taking just Moon, who wound up being a goal judge in Boston. He went over with them and they ended up in second place.

While all this was going on I became more and more interested in the science of hockey and its equipment and was lucky in a couple of ways. I got to be very good friends with Lester Patrick, and whenever I had an idea I knew I could get a good ear from him. One day I went up to him and said, "Lester, it's kind of ridiculous to wear elbow pads on the outside of a hockey jersey, isn't it?"

He agreed but wanted to know what I could do about it. "I'll tell you what," I suggested, "I could build a jersey that would have elbow pads underneath."

He said, "Do it!" I did and that's how all the pros started wearing their elbow pads out of sight. But I wasn't even beginning to get into the equipment business yet. After all, I still wanted to play hockey and was gaining so much self-confidence I felt I could do better than just be a practice goalie. By 1939 I figured I was good enough to play for the Rovers, the Rangers' farm team in the Eastern League, and a damn good one at that; I mean, guys like the Colville brothers actually went up to the NHL from the Rovers. Tom Lockhart let me be their sub goalie and I played a few games for them when their regular, Johnny Fisher, got hurt.

In 1940, the Rovers opened the season with Jack McGill in goal. He was a funny one, always in the nets with a white towel around his neck. But he had a bad knee and after a while I was the goalie again. In 1940 that was one of the best Rovers teams they ever had. I remember playing five games in one week and winning all of them. We won the league that year and I played most of the games. As a goalie I talked a lot and wouldn't accept anyone out there who wouldn't backcheck; if they didn't backcheck, I let them know right on the ice.

Playing for the Rovers that year changed my whole life, but I didn't realize it at the time. One day Tommy Lockhart called me into his office to ask a simple question: "Can you get me a gross of hockey sticks?"

If I'd said no, I wouldn't be running the biggest hockey equipment company in the world. But the answer was "yes," and the next thing I knew I was on the phone with a company in Erie, Pennsylvania, and managed to get Lockhart a gross of sticks at a very good price. It must have been good because he came back to me right away for more, then he wanted some gloves and pads. That started me in the hockey equipment business in 1940.

By now I was getting enough orders from Lockhart—and from the Rangers and Americans—to make me think of opening a store. Well, since I had an apartment on York Avenue in Manhattan, I put aside a little room there for equipment and was off and running.

Meantime, I was still playing hockey for the Rovers and wherever else Lockhart wanted me to go. And, as I said, I was expanding my equipment business. Lockhart was terrific, except for one thing: he liked quality in all kinds of equipment but pucks. I could never understand why he had this thing about buying pucks harder than rocks with edges like razor blades.

He'd pay about seven cents apiece for them, and if a goalie got hit in the face with those edges it was too bad—I know. Once in a game against Washington that team was taking unbelievable shots on me, and in one rush my defenseman kept backing up on top of me. Meanwhile, the Washington forward wound up and shot, and the puck deflected off my defenseman's stick and caught me on the side of the face. That sharp edge hit my cheek so hard it actually ripped a hole right in my face, and I can remember coming to and sticking my tongue right out through the hole. They sewed me up in the infirmary and I went back in and finished the game.

If you think that's crazy, you've got to remember that hockey players are different from other athletes. Take a baseball player: if he gets a hangnail he's moaning and groaning and probably stays out for three weeks. But hockey players have always been a breed apart, mainly because they're disciplined. Most of them have come from hard-working families and if they didn't do what they were supposed to, they'd hear about it. To me, they're the greatest people in the world, the most down-to-earth of all athletes.

Well, as I was saying, Lockhart gave me more and more business, both on and off the ice. I was handling the two NHL teams, the Eastern League teams, and eventually, the Met League clubs that played out of Madison Square Garden, and on the ice, Tom really worked me. By 1942 the war was on and lots of players had left for the Army. One was Vic Polich, goalie for the Boston Olympics in the Eastern League.

When Vic left the club, Boston was in real trouble because they couldn't come up with a substitute, and that's when I got another distinction. I was the only guy to play on two teams in the same league at the same time, and believe me, it wasn't easy! At that same time we would often play in Washington on, say Wednesday night, and take the train back to New York sometime on Thursday. Then Lockhart would discover that the Olympics needed me that night—in Washington, of all places.

Soon I was playing more hockey than I had ever played in my life and also doing more business with equipment. The York Avenue apartment wasn't large enough anymore so I moved to a bigger place, opposite Rockefeller Center. Then I got lucky again. At one time I had arranged an audition for the daughter of Frank O'Shea, a big sporting goods dealer in Chicago. O'Shea remembered that favor and when he decided to close his business he called me and sold me 27 cases of equipment. I didn't know it then but that equipment was a goldmine, because after the war broke out you couldn't buy stuff like that; it kept business going all during the war.

Hockey has come a long way. Above all, the game is so much faster and the plays are actually better. I saw a play made by Rod Gilbert, Jean Ratelle, and Vic Hadfield one night that was so fast I was glad I wasn't tending goal. In the old days Frankie Boucher would take the puck up center ice and would have all the time in the world to make a pass. Nobody would bother him and he'd pass through the defenseman's legs and Bill or Bun Cook would be flying in on the wings, take the pass, and skate in for a shot on goal. To be a goaltender today you've got to be really super. So many screened shots alone are murder, not to mention the slap shots. A guy has to have great reflexes to be a modern goalie.

chapter five

Babe Pratt
The Most Colorful Ranger

BORN: Stony Mountain, Manitoba, January 7, 1916

DIED: December 16, 1988

POSITION: Defenseman, New York Rangers, 1935–43; Toronto Maple Leafs, 1943–46; Boston Bruins, 1946–47

AWARDS/HONORS: Hart Memorial Trophy, 1944; NHL All-Star, 1944; NHL Second Team All-Star, 1945; Hockey Hall of Fame, 1966

Babe Pratt in some ways resembled a baseball Babe, and not the one named Ruth. The Brooklyn Dodgers boasted a star named Babe Herman, a formidable hitter whose ability was often overshadowed by his zany antics.

And that was the story of Babe Pratt's hockey life.

Enormously talented, rugged on defense yet creative on offense as well, Pratt and his Stanley Cup heroics occasionally were overshadowed by his comic personality. Some of Pratt's off-ice antics are better remembered than the fact that he scored the Stanley Cup–winning goal for the Toronto Maple Leafs in Game 7 in 1945.

Long before that Pratt had starred for seven years on Broadway and was a major factor for coach Frank Boucher's Blueshirts when New York won the Stanley Cup in 1940. I was an Eastern District High School sophomore in Brooklyn when Pratt retired in 1947 as a member of the Boston Bruins and I never had a chance to meet him firsthand until long after his retirement.

But stories about the Babe arrested my attention, and in 1968 I finally had an opportunity to meet him.

It was the year of my marriage to Shirley Walton, whose family had lived in Washington State and, briefly, the Canadian province of British Columbia.

During our vacation that summer we motored north to Canada with stops in Vancouver and then New Westminster. My goal was to interview as many Hockey Hall of Famers as possible, and when I discovered that Pratt worked for a lumber company in New Westminster, I phoned him and he obliged by inviting Shirley and me to his office at the mill.

This was old-time stuff, reminding me of the early lumbering days on the Pacific Coast.

From his window the then 52-year-old Pratt had a clear view of a log-filled river.

Occasionally he'd peer out to check on the lumber but for several hours he regaled us with stories of his days as a Rangers hero.

Our oral history begins in Pratt's home city, Winnipeg, Manitoba, which once was the Blueshirts training camp and also sponsored its Junior team, the Winnipeg Rangers.

Winnipeg, which is where I grew up, was a terrific hockey town; they had great teams there going back to the 19th century and always seemed to be winning the Allan Cup for supremacy in Senior amateur hockey. There were also several Winnipeg teams that received the Memorial Cup for the Canadian Junior championship.

In those early days of pro hockey I think Winnipeg Amphitheater had the only artificial ice plant outside of Toronto. In fact, the city was such a hotbed of hockey that when I was a kid they had a saying: no matter where you were in the world you could find a Swedish match, an English sailor, a German whore, and a hockey player from Winnipeg.

I wasn't the first hockey player in my family; my older brother was pretty good but he was even better as a soccer player. And in those days a fellow could make more money in soccer than hockey, so he went to England and played there. But then he found out he could get paid even more money in Scotland for playing hockey, so he wound up in that country. He might even have made it as an NHL player but he never cared about hockey as much as I did.

Naturally, we had a lot of hockey heroes in Winnipeg; mine was Frank Frederickson, who had come from Iceland and lived near us. I watched Frank play and felt I wanted to be just like him. Luckily, it was easy to practice in Winnipeg since we had something like 64 rinks for kids 12 years old and under.

We always played outdoors on natural ice and there was no problem in getting the ice because it would get as cold as 30 or 40 degrees below zero. Our games were held every Saturday morning and I can remember some of them vividly. In fact, I recall how we won the championship, even though we got beaten 8–0 in the final game. We had found out that there were six guys on the other team who were overage, so they forfeited to us. The following year we played in the playground league and got beaten legitimately.

When I reached the age of 15 I began to play for real winners. I was one of the Junior champions of Manitoba, and even though I played defense I led the league in scoring. As a puck-carrier I was pretty good; any time I had the puck I'd go down the ice with it, something like a Bobby Orr.

There wasn't enough hockey around for me to play—that's how much I loved it. Once, I played four games in one day. Between noon and 1:00 PM I played for the high school; at 4:30 I had a game at another high school; at 7:00 that night I played in the church league; and there was a taxi waiting to take me to an 8:30 game, played at 30 degrees below zero. I think I won every game that day.

On nights when there weren't regular league games we'd have to wait until the public skating sessions were over in the local rinks. Usually it would be about 10:00 at night before we were able to get on the ice. My father often came down to watch me; he loved hockey. Lester Patrick always said that an athlete's greatest asset is healthy parents; I was lucky enough to have them.

I eventually went to Kenora, a town in Western Ontario not that far from Winnipeg, and played Junior hockey there. There are lots of Indians in that area and my coach was a full-blooded one named Sandy Sanderson. He was a fine coach with a great compassion for youngsters, something that's missing today. All we seem to have in Junior hockey coaches nowadays is a bunch of fellows who want to do nothing but win and send players to the big leagues, completely ignoring character-building in the boys. They're so interested in

Seen here as a member of the Toronto Maple Leafs, Babe Pratt was a Stanley Cup champion with the Rangers in 1940.

pushing into the majors that they do not have the understanding to work with the player who isn't that good.

When I played in Kenora I was scouted by Al Ritchie, who worked for the New York Rangers. Lester Patrick was then the Rangers boss and he was to hockey what John McGraw was to baseball. Lester had friends everywhere in Western Canada; when any of his buddies saw a hockey player he thought might make a good pro he'd get in touch with Lester, who would send his head scout, Al Ritchie, out to investigate. Well, Al told many people I was the greatest prospect he'd ever scouted and invited me to the New York Rangers training camp in 1934.

Lester had asked 23 amateurs to that camp and, as things turned out, 16 of them made it to the big leagues. Neil and Mac Colville, Alex Shibicky, Bert Gardiner, Joe Cooper, Lynn and Muzz Patrick, Don Metz, Phil Watson, and Mel Hill were there, among others. At the time, Lester wanted me to turn pro but I still had two years of Junior hockey left. Then he got stuck because two of his regulars, Ching Johnson and Earl Seibert, were holding out for more dough and he needed an extra defenseman to work out with the team. He asked me to stay with the club and I worked out with the Rangers for 10 days.

After practicing with Bill and Bun Cook and Frank Boucher, I really felt I belonged with the big club. However, I decided to go back and play Junior hockey for another year—and it was a fabulous one. Our team finished first and I led the league in scoring with 20 points.

The next fall I went back to the New York training camp and turned pro with the Rangers, although Lester farmed me out to Philadelphia for two months along with the Colvilles, Shibicky, and Phil Watson. That was the first year the Rangers didn't make the playoffs, but the following year Lester got together a sprinkling of old-timers—Boucher, Johnson, Murray Murdoch, and Butch Keeling—and a bunch of youngsters, and we made the playoffs easily. We reached the Stanley Cup Finals only to get beaten in the fifth game of a three-out-of-five series.

From that point on Lester went with youth. He brought up Bryan Hextall, Art Coulter, Clint Smith, and, in the following year, Muzz Patrick. When I started playing with the Rangers, Lester alternately teamed me with Ching Johnson, Art Coulter, and Ott Heller.

By the end of the 1930s Patrick had really developed a powerful hockey club; we could play terrifically, offensively as well as defensively. Conn Smythe, who was then running the Toronto Maple Leafs, said that the 1940 Rangers were the greatest hockey club he'd ever seen. In those days, whenever we came to Toronto, Smythe would advertise us as "The Broadway Blues, Hockey's Classiest Team."

Our club was so well balanced that our first line scored 38 goals, the second, 37, and the third line, 36, over the season.

On that Rangers team we had three great centermen—Clint Smith, Phil Watson, and Neil Colville—plus so many good wingmen that we were able to put the pressure on the other team when we were a man short. Our power play was so strong that once the Toronto Maple Leafs took a penalty we kept the puck in their end of the rink for the entire two minutes—and scored two goals.

It was a different kind of game then. Today, they stress boardchecking and checking from behind, both unheard of when we played. We'd hit a man standing right up and now the players don't seem to want to take that kind of check. The only check they want is on the first and 15th of the month.

Sure, we played a tough game but we also had a million laughs. There was a newspaperman from *The New York World Telegram* named Jim Burchard who liked to drink, tell stories, and do wild things like swim across the Hudson River. Once, we had Ukulele Ike traveling with us and, naturally, Burchard had his own ukulele that he played every night we were in a Stanley Cup round. We also had quite a few jokers on the team. Ching Johnson was one; he was also one of the finest players when it came to working with rookies. Ching was also from Winnipeg, and he sort of took me under his wing.

That was quite unusual when you consider Ching was getting old and was on his way out of the NHL and I would be the one to take his place. Of course, you can never take the place of a great athlete who retires; you simply do the job in your own way. Ching was not what you'd call a "picture player"—he wasn't a beautiful passer or stickhandler—but he was one of the hardest hitters in the history of the game, a great leader, and an absolute bulwark on defense.

He'd hit a man and grin from ear to ear and he'd be that way in the dressing room, too. There was never a time when Ching didn't have itching powder in his pocket, ready for a practical joke. One time he gave Lester Patrick a hotfoot and Lester's shoe caught on fire; Lester was half asleep at the time and after they put out the fire he couldn't walk for a week. It took a lot of nerve to do that to Lester Patrick.

Of all the players on the Rangers, Muzz Patrick became my closest friend; he was the flamboyant type, and I was no little Lord Fauntleroy, either. In fact, Lester classified me as "Peck's Bad Boy" from the time I joined the team. I remember when Lester came to Winnipeg and a little redcap said to him, "God, you kept Pratt in terrific shape, he ain't had a drink all summer." Lester answered, "I think that's marvelous for a 17-year-old boy!"

Lester reacted to Muzz the way he did to me. Once Muzz's name appeared in Walter Winchell's column; it was about his being in the company of a beautiful showgirl. Shortly thereafter we had a meeting and Lester threw the paper over asking Muzz if he'd seen the item.

Muzz looked at it for a few seconds, then replied, "Isn't that marvelous, Lester? And very well written." Knowing his father, Muzz anticipated that Lester would harangue him about the article, so he said, "Lester, I just want to ask you something: how many hockey players have ever made Winchell's column?"

"None," Lester answered. Muzz smiled and said, "Well, I'm getting you the greatest publicity you've ever had." At that point, Lester thought about it for a moment, then admitted, "You got me pal, you got me."

Both of Lester's sons, Muzz and Lynn, were with the Rangers at the same time and in one way it was quite a handicap to them. People would keep mentioning Lester and Frank Patrick to the young guys and reminisce about how great they were.

On the other hand, Lynn and Muzz got a lot of help from their father. I always look at it this way: if your father isn't going to help you, who is? It's the same in almost any business controlled by a family—it's handed down to the sons. You don't see a Rockefeller digging ditches.

Even though he called me "Peck's Bad Boy," Lester liked me and I loved playing in New York. It was a great hockey town then and still is. Lester made sure that the new Rangers appreciated the place. He'd tell them, "Where's Helen Hayes? Where's John Barrymore? Where are all the great stage actors? The great singers and the Metropolitan Opera? Where does anybody go who's any good? What do they do? They go to New York."

But you can't sell a kid a bill of goods like that anymore. He'll just turn around and say, "I'll go where the dollars are." If they're in Manitoba, that's where he'll play.

After a while, though, I think Lester got a bit disturbed at some of my extra-curricular activities. I was having fun but I got hurt during World War II when talent was scarce, and he had an opportunity to make a deal with Toronto whereby he'd get two players for me. Since the team wasn't winning I was expendable; that's how I wound up with the Leafs.

As it turned out I went from one great character to another, Conn Smythe, the Leafs manager. I guess Conn was the greatest exhorter hockey has ever known. And he had the greatest coach in Hap Day. What made things really unusual was that I was the only player in hockey to room with his coach.

You know, lots of people think that happened because then I'd be under the coach's thumb, but I didn't feel that way. I always thought Hap was a lonely man who needed my company. In any event, I had some great times with the Leafs. I won the Hart Trophy as the NHL's Most Valuable Player and got 57 points in 50 games as a defenseman; it was 20 years before that record was broken by Pierre Pilote of the Chicago Black Hawks. He scored 59 points in 68 games.

But I guess my greatest thrill was beating Detroit for the Stanley Cup in 1945. You have to remember that in 1942, Toronto had lost three straight games in the Finals to Detroit, then bounced back to take the next four—the only time that ever happened in Cup play. In 1945 the Leafs won the first three and lost the next three to Detroit. I'll always remember the seventh, deciding game.

It was in Detroit and whenever we played there we usually left for the rink at about 7:30 PM. I was rooming with Hap Day as usual and was snoring away when Hap came in and kicked me right out of bed. I woke up on the floor, looked up, and said, "What the hell's with you, Hap?"

"How can you sleep when the final Cup game is going to start in less than an hour," he demanded. "How can you do it?"

"Well, Hap," I said, "it's simply because the game doesn't start until 8:30. That's when I'll go to work."

He wasn't upset anymore. "Well, Babe," he replied, "I'll tell you one thing, you were never short on building yourself up, so I'll look forward to a good game from you."

The score was tied in the third period when Detroit had a man off with a penalty. I started toward the Red Wings net and took a pass from Nick Metz, a great but underrated player. Harry Lumley was the goalie for Detroit and Earl Siebert and Flash Hollett were on defense. When I got the puck I skated in from the point, made a double-pass with Metz, and received it back on my stick. I slid a long one into the corner of the net—it turned out to be the winning goal.

I always felt that if any one person could have been given the Stanley Cup to keep for himself that year, Hap Day should have gotten it for the way he handled our club. We had great goaltending from Frank McCool plus some good players like Wally Stanowski, Elwin Morris, Gus Bodnar, Teeder Kennedy, and Mel Hill. But, to me, Hap Day was the man who made it all work.

During the 1946–47 season, the Leafs traded me to the Boston Bruins, a move I considered very fortunate. Winding up with a club like Boston was discouraging; still, I had a chance to play with the Kraut Line of Milt Schmidt, Woody Dumart, and Bobby Bauer, and with guys like Bill Cowley, Dit Clapper, and Johnny Crawford. The Bruins' problem was that they never practiced. With a team like Toronto I could keep my weight down because we worked out every day for two hours; in Boston, I had no control over my weight and was never in the condition I used to be. This hurt me and I became susceptible to injuries. I always feel that when a player gets hurt it's usually because he's not in shape.

In my case, Art Ross, the Boston manager, sent me down to the minors for a couple of weeks, thinking I'd come right back. But I arrived in Hershey and got injured again, and when it came time to return to the Bruins I was in the hospital, so they took somebody else instead.

On the other hand it was somewhat fortunate that I stayed there because the Bears won the American League championship and we got $1,800 apiece as a playoff check, while Boston got beaten in the first round of the playoffs and I think their players received only $600.

I never did play in the NHL again. In 1947–48 I spent part of the season in Cleveland, then in 1948–49 I went west to play three seasons for New Westminster in the Pacific Coast Hockey League. My last year was with Tacoma in 1951–52.

Over the years I saw a lot of hockey and many good hockey players. Looking back, I'd say that Milt Schmidt of the Boston Bruins had the most drive. Schmidt, Syl Apps of the Maple Leafs, and Neil Colville of the Rangers were the three greatest puck-carriers I've ever seen. Of course the greatest goal-scorer was Rocket Richard, but he wasn't the greatest player; to me that was Jean Beliveau. He was a polished performer who did everything—stickhandle, shoot, the works! As for the smaller men, Stan Mikita of the Black Hawks is a little guy who could shoot the way Doug Bentley used to and make plays like Bill Cowley did for Boston. However, Little Stan was a hundred percent for himself, whereas these other guys were more team men.

Looking back at the defensemen, Doug Harvey ranks as the greatest along with "Black" Jack Stewart, who played for the Red Wings and the Black Hawks. Stewart never was the puck-carrier that Harvey was; just a real, fine, sound defenseman.

If you ask me, today's game could be improved with a rule change here and there. I'd love to see them do away with the blue line; I really think this would open up the game.

I'd also like to see the nets put right in the backboard. That would eliminate the habit modern defensemen have of going behind the net and standing there. With everything in front of them they'd have to go up the ice with the puck and this would also stop a lot of that bodychecking behind the nets. The puck would be alive and there'd be more sustained action.

Let's face it, the game is different today and so are the players. In my day you had to be able to stickhandle; some of these fellows I see now couldn't stickhandle past their mothers without losing the puck, and some couldn't pass it to their mother if she were starving to death and it was a piece of bread they were handing her.

But they do a heck of a job on defense by slamming into guys, going down, and stopping pucks. They earn their money there; but for real hockey—the way the fundamentals were originally taught by people like Lester Patrick and Art Ross—these fellows playing today can't do the job.

When I played we were taught not to shoot the puck until we saw the whites of the goaltender's eyes. Now they blast from anywhere, hoping the puck will hit somebody's skates or ankles and bounce into the net. And when they go to sign next year's contract the manager never asks whether the player stickhandled through the whole team, faked the goaltender, and tucked the puck in the net; all he says is, "How many did you get?"

Another difference is that the modern players don't have the laughs we used to; and that includes the hockey writers, too. Believe it or not, I once wrote a story for Burchard in the *World Telegram*. We'd been playing the Maple Leafs in the playoffs and Toronto had just brought up a rookie named Hank Goldup. After one of the games, Bouchard came over to me and said, "Babe, make me my story. C'mon, write it for me."

I said, "I was on the ice the same time as Goldup and it was the first time I played against him. I wanted to see if he could shoot. He did, and he scored the winning goal." The next night I picked up the paper and there was the headline: PRATT FINDS OUT ROOKIE CAN SHOOT, POPS IN WINNER. I was only kidding around and Burchard made me the goof on the play.

One year—I think 1936—the writers were the ones who gave out assists on goals, something like official scorers in baseball today. They were so funny—they once gave *three* assists on one goal.

As I said, things were different then; even the arenas have changed. They used to be noisy and the fans were closer to the ice, now they're big and new but they're not the same. I went to the opening of the new Madison Square Garden and when I got inside I looked around and thought, *Jesus, this is a cold-looking joint.*

The crowds have changed, too. You don't get the same funny cracks we used to, especially from the gallery gods. I remember once at the Garden there was a game with the Red Wings who we were beating 6–1. Jack Adams, Detroit's manager, had just gotten his citizenship papers and suddenly a fan yelled out, "Hey, Adams, it's a good thing you got citizenship; now you can get home relief!"

Another time we were leading the Americans by about six goals. A voice from the stands yelled down to me, "Hey, Walter, why don't you turn the net around; nobody's looking!"

The attitudes have changed; everything is all business. When a hockey player gets on a plane he's as apt to pick up *The Wall Street Journal* as anything else. And when business gets more important than the sport itself, that's not right.

chapter six

Bill Chadwick

The Almost Ranger Who Became a Hall of Fame Referee

BORN: New York, New York, October 10, 1915

DIED: October 24, 2009

POSITION: Referee, 1941–55

AWARDS/HONORS: Hockey Hall of Fame, 1964; United States Hockey Hall of Fame, 1974

Had luck been on his side, Bill Chadwick might have been the first New York City product to become a Rangers star.

As it happened the Jamaica High School graduate became a Metropolitan League ace and graduated to the Rangers farm team, the New York Rovers, in the highly competitive Eastern League. But two serious hockey accidents got in the way, leaving Chadwick with sight in only his left eye.

When it was apparent that his playing career was over, Rangers executive Tom Lockhart—he also ran the Eastern League—urged Chadwick to take up refereeing. And thus a Hall of Fame career was born. First, in the Eastern League and then in 1941 in the NHL.

Because he was known as a native New Yorker, Chadwick became a favorite among Rangers fans. And after his retirement as an official he became even more beloved by the Blueshirts faithful as a Rangers broadcaster.

Working with play-by-play man Marv Albert, Chadwick became known on the airwaves as the "Big Whistle."

Over time, Chadwick emerged as a colorful broadcaster often intruding very personal commentary. After the Rangers acquired highly touted defenseman Barry Beck, Chadwick would lament over the air that Beck failed to use his best weapon: his shot.

"Shoot the puck, Barry! Shoot the puck!" was a frequently heard demand by Chadwick, which soon was taken up by thousands of New York fans.

Or when speedy prospect Gene Carr failed to capitalize on many scoring chances, Chadwick liked to comment, "That guy couldn't shoot the puck in the ocean if he was standing right on an Atlantic pier!"

I met Chadwick, person to person, in 1954 when I began working for the Rangers, and our friendship lasted through his retirement and through his broadcasting career.

I did several interviews with the Big Whistle including a television feature for SportsChannel.

Since I, too, am a native New Yorker, I had a special interest in Bill's success and was tickled to do an oral history with him.

What follows picks up with Bill's first introduction to organized hockey in the Big Apple.

I was different from most of the people involved with the NHL because I grew up in New York City and learned my hockey there. That was in the 1930s when there weren't many indoor rinks around and not enough cold weather for much outdoor ice.

Luckily, I went to Jamaica High School in Queens, one of the few city schools with an ice hockey team. I had always loved to skate and my father had bought me a pair of long racing skates. When they had tryouts for the team I showed up with the racers and they told me to beat it; I borrowed a pair of hockey skates and then made the team.

We used to play a lot of games at the Brooklyn Ice Palace, an old rink near the railroad tracks in the Bedford-Stuyvesant section. Manual Training High School, Brooklyn Tech, and Brooklyn Prep were some of the other clubs. We won the championship and I went on to play for the Floral Park Maroons, a pretty good amateur team. In those days amateur hockey was really big in

New York and the top teams were in the Metropolitan League. They played their games on Sunday afternoons at Madison Square Garden before the New York Rovers games. It was quite common to draw crowds of from 12,000 to 15,000 fans on any given Sunday and, naturally, it was a great thrill to play there.

One Met League team was called the Stock Exchange Brokers. It was backed by some sports enthusiasts on Wall Street and guys who played for the club usually got jobs on the Exchange. Somebody on Wall Street offered me a job as well as the chance to play hockey and baseball; that's how I got into organized hockey and eventually to the NHL.

I was 10 years old when I started skating. We'd go to Central Park when it froze over or to the Brooklyn Ice Palace for the regular sessions. So I had done quite a bit of skating in my early days, and even before I got the job on the Exchange I was so enthused about hockey I used to play for a couple of teams while I still was going to high school. One of them was the Jamaica Hawks, in the Met League, and the other was Fordham University's team. I played for Jamaica under the name of O'Donoghue and as Flanigan with Fordham.

But when I got the job on Wall Street I played for the Exchange Brokers under my own name and began to play quite well. All during my high school days I had been a Rangers fan and used to sit in the gallery rooting for the Cook Brothers, hoping that maybe, someday, I might make it to the NHL. But then an accident changed my career.

I was 19 at the time—it was March 1935—and I was selected to play on the Metropolitan League's All-Star Team that was playing similar teams from other East Coast cities. One afternoon our opponent was Boston and that's when I got hurt.

The Boston team was out warming up when we left our dressing room. Just as I stepped onto the ice somebody on Boston shot the puck and it hit me smack in the right eye.

When I regained consciousness, they took me out of Madison Square Garden to the hospital. After two weeks several doctors decided there was no way of restoring the sight in my right eye. Eventually, they released me from the hospital and I went right back to playing hockey the next fall. It was odd because I had tried to play baseball after the accident and found that I'd misjudge the ball after it bounced and really couldn't play the game anymore the way I used to. However, I felt I could still make the same judgments in hockey as before.

I couldn't have been too bad because in 1936 I was picked to play for the New York Rovers, the Rangers farm team in the fast Eastern League. This was really something because many players went from the Rovers to high pro leagues and some even went to the NHL where they became stars.

I played center for the Rovers in 1936 and was back with them at the start of 1937, then the second accident happened. This time it was in a Rovers game and I got hit by a puck or a stick, I can't remember which, in the left eye. The blood started trickling into my eye and soon my vision was gone. Fortunately, it cleared up and I was able to see out of the eye again but decided that I'd had enough as a hockey player.

Tommy Lockhart, who was president of the Amateur Hockey Association of the United States, also ran the Rovers at that time and, of course, he knew I had sight in only one eye. As a matter of fact, until the second accident I was the only one in the league wearing a helmet; I wore it far down on my forehead, trying to protect my good eye.

Well, after the accidents I still came regularly to the Sunday afternoon Rovers games at Madison Square Garden. One afternoon in March 1937, I was at the Garden when somebody mentioned that the referee wasn't going to appear because of a snowstorm that was blowing outside. Lockhart spotted me in the stands and said, "Bill, will you fill in?" I was glad to and Tom must have liked what he saw because he then asked me to become a regular referee in the Metropolitan League. He also said he wanted me to be a linesman for the Eastern League games.

At the time all the players in the league knew I had only one good eye but nobody gave me any trouble about it. In fact, right from the start I thought I had a psychological advantage and consequently was a better official. You see, because I was using only one eye that fact was always on my mind and it made me work harder than the other fellows. I skated harder and was closer to the play; in most cases I was on top of it. Pretty soon Lockhart asked me to be in the Eastern League, which led to my being picked as a linesman for the NHL. Actually, I almost quit before making it to the NHL; if I had, I would never have been named to the Hockey Hall of Fame.

What caused me to think of quitting was a game at a rink in River Vale, New Jersey, about an hour or so from New York City. There was a team there called the River Vale Skeeters and its manager, John Handwerg, really gave me the business that Saturday night for the way I was officiating. I was so mad after it was over I went to Lockhart and said, "I'm finished! I'm never going to referee again."

Remember, this was on a Saturday night. The following Wednesday I got a wire from Frank Calder, president of the NHL, appointing me a big-league linesman. This was quite a shock but I was told that Red Dutton, who ran the New York Americans, and Lockhart were behind it all.

Officiating was different at that time. It was customary to have "hometown linesmen;" that is, linesmen from each city would handle games for teams in their city. This meant there were linesmen who worked only the Rangers games and those who'd handle the Americans. I was the linesman for the Americans.

It wasn't very long before I was in trouble. In one of my first games the Americans were playing the Montreal Canadiens at Madison Square Garden. At the time the NHL used one referee and one linesman. Bill Stewart, who was such a great baseball umpire, was the referee then. During the game the Canadiens manager, Cecil Hart, gave us a real hard time; and here I was, a kid of 22, and this was all new to me. As soon as the game ended Stewart said, "Follow me!" So I followed him and he walked right into the Canadiens dressing room to challenge Hart. I knew then what refereeing was all about. Of course, nothing really came of it. Hart just brushed him off because Stewart was a bit of a hothead who felt nobody could criticize what he was doing.

Whether Stewart eventually retired on his own or not I don't know, but in 1941 I was appointed a referee in the NHL. Calder made the official appointment but he was fronting for the governors. In those days somebody else made the bullets and he fired them.

Whatever the case, everybody on the Board of Governors knew I only had one eye but never said anything about it. I decided to ignore the matter and everything moved smoothly until I crossed the Detroit Red Wings.

It was really strange because up until then I had been the fair-haired boy in Detroit. Jack Adams was the Detroit manager and he was a roly-poly, tough little guy. The Red Wings were a powerful organization and the feeling was that if you called one wrong against Adams in Detroit—or one that *he* thought was wrong—you were a goner, because each club owner carried so much power. Apparently, if you didn't satisfy them they'd get rid of you. If you check the records, you'll see that few officials lasted very long then.

In my case the thing that annoyed Adams was a call I made in the seventh game of the Stanley Cup Finals between Detroit and Toronto. A few years earlier they had played in the Finals and Detroit had won the first three games. Then Toronto bounced back to win the next four. Well, this time it looked like the reverse. Toronto won the first three—all on shutouts by goalie Frank McCool—then Detroit won the next three. So there we were in the seventh game at Olympia Stadium in Detroit, and I'm the referee.

My problems started when I called a big penalty against Syd Howe of the Red Wings. He had crosschecked Gus Bodnar with a few minutes left in the game and the score tied 1–1. While Howe was in the penalty box Babe Pratt of Toronto scored the winning goal and Toronto got the Stanley Cup.

That infuriated Adams and Jim Norris, the Red Wings owner. From that time on every year I'd be sent for an eye examination, and in my opinion it was at Norris' instigation.

Actually, the fact that Jim Norris and Adams weren't fond of me was the greatest thing that ever happened because it meant that the other five governors were for me. But don't think I wasn't still under a lot of pressure. We all were, except that officials felt it differently than they do today.

One big difference was that the dressing room of the referee and linesman stood practically open to the coaches and managers. As a result they'd almost wait in line outside just to get in and intimidate us. There was no such thing as keeping your door closed. After every period somebody would come in, complaining or bitching and trying to intimidate. Nowadays, though, the referees have all the protection in the world.

Meanwhile I was going along and doing my best. Ironically, every so often some fan in the balcony would yell down at me, "Chadwick, you blind bastard," and I'd chuckle to myself because I knew they were half right.

My condition didn't hamper me. I had 20-20 vision in my good left eye and was on top of the play even more than they are now. I was never away from the net when there was a play on goal and I didn't have much trouble from the players, except for a few.

Maurice Richard of the Canadiens and Ted Lindsay of the Red Wings gave me the toughest time, although I never thought they were picking just on me. I believe it was because of their personal makeup and their character; they would have done it to *anybody.*

Richard was possibly the fiercest competitor I've ever seen in any sport. If you weren't playing on the same team with Maurice Richard you were his enemy, and that applied to you if you were a referee giving him penalties. I remember being at a Lester Patrick Trophy dinner once, on the dais with some of the all-time great hockey players including Richard and Milt Schmidt. I tried to get an autograph for my son from everybody there. I asked Schmidt for his and, naturally, he gave it to me. Richard was beside Schmidt so I asked him next. "I give you no autograph. You only give me penalties!" he replied. He was serious; it wasn't any joke with Richard, and I wound up without his autograph.

Because of the way Richard and Lindsay were on the ice I had a special thing I'd do with them at the start of every season, and to this day I'm not sure whether I did it purposely or not. In the first three or four games of every season I'd give Richard and Lindsay misconduct penalties. I'd do it right away, because if I didn't, they might think I wasn't their boss. I had to assert myself early and it was easier to do it then instead of later on in the middle of the season or at the end.

I'm pretty damn sure Richard and Lindsay knew I had only one good eye, especially with guys like Jack Adams in Detroit and Frank Selke in Montreal. And there *was* one time when the fact actually busted out in print. It was in a Detroit paper when I was asking for a two-week draft deferment to allow me to clear up the Stanley Cup playoffs before being drafted into World War II. The headline in the paper read, "ONE EYED REFEREE ASKS FOR DRAFT DEFERMENT." But nobody else ever picked it up, not even the New York papers.

As it turned out I wasn't drafted and I continued refereeing, liking it more and more. Lots of fascinating things happened, like the 1946–47 season when Richard lost the Stanley Cup for the Canadiens all by himself. Montreal was playing Toronto in the Finals and I was refereeing. In one of the early games Richard cut Vic Lynn of Toronto and I gave him a five-minute major penalty. Later in the game he got into a fight with Bill Ezinicki of the

Known among Rangers fans as the "Big Whistle," Bill Chadwick became a beloved broadcaster after his career as a hockey referee ended.

Leafs. In those days it was the referee who separated fighting players, not the linesman, and so I went in between them, but Richard reached over my shoulder and cut Ezinicki in the middle of the head. That meant a 10-minute match penalty, whereby the team had to play shorthanded for 10 minutes. Toronto won that game and league president Clarence Campbell suspended Richard for the next game, and Toronto went on to capture the Stanley Cup.

During the mid- and late-1940s there was an occasional suggestion that I leaned over to give the Rangers a hard time. On the one hand I was accused of being a "homer" with the Rangers because I lived in New York; otherwise I wasn't one and was out to prove it by calling them hard on the Rangers. One thing I know for sure: I wasn't a homer anywhere I worked. I would have quit refereeing if I was considered such. I can't say I was extra hard on New York, especially if you consider that in the days I refereed in the NHL the Rangers didn't have much of a hockey club. And it wasn't my fault. Surprisingly, I never had a tough time in Montreal. I'm smug enough to think that I did well there because the fans know the game. Likewise, I was always well received in Toronto. But the toughest place was Chicago and I don't know why. I just never felt comfortable in that big Chicago Stadium.

Now, don't get the impression I never made a mistake. I'm a great believer in God Almighty and I think he's the only one who never makes a mistake. I made plenty. One of them made me a better official in the eyes of NHL people. It happened during a playoff game between Boston and Montreal. At the time Lynn Patrick was coaching the Bruins and we had a delayed penalty ruling. This means the referee holds off blowing the whistle if the offended team has the puck. What happened was that Doug Mohns of Boston was fouled just as he shot the puck, and instead of delaying my whistle, I blew it immediately, thus halting play. Mohns' shot went into the net but the goal was disallowed since I had mistakenly blown the whistle.

If the goal had counted it would have tied the game and given Boston a good chance at winning, and of course Lynn Patrick raised Cain about it from the bench. Finally, I skated alongside him and said, "Lynn, I made a mistake. I can't breathe in after it. I made a mistake."

After the game Patrick came into the officials' dressing room and said he'd never criticize me again since I was big enough to admit my error. But mistakes are part of the game and it really was a great life. I refereed for six months and had the other six off. That's why I remained for 16 years in the NHL as a referee. I decided to quit in 1955 at the age of 39 because I believe an athlete, whether a participant or an official, should stop while he's on top. Five years after I retired I was elected to the Hockey Hall of Fame.

If I had stayed on as a referee—I think I was capable of five more years—possibly I'd have been asked to leave and been given a cushy job someplace, and I'm not the type who can take that. I didn't want anybody to give me anything; I wanted to earn it. In retrospect I think it all worked out well and I have no regrets about my officiating. I learned a lot over those years. In order for a referee to be good he must have the respect of the players, and even though Richard and Lindsay gave me a rough time, I'm sure they respected me.

The trick was to gain the regard of the older players on each team—the leaders. It couldn't be done in a year or two. When I refereed I think I got away with more on the ice than any of my colleagues because I had the players' esteem. I could make a call that a new guy, who didn't have the players' respect, couldn't get away with, without getting the business.

Remember, I refereed for three NHL presidents: Frank Calder, Red Dutton, and Clarence Campbell. Calder was a gentleman, whereas Dutton was one of the rabble-rousers of the NHL. In fact, when he was a manager he would lead the parades to our dressing room to protest decisions, but as president he was all for the referees—except once.

Around 1944, during a game between the Black Hawks and Canadiens in Chicago, the score was tied 2–2 when Chicago's George Allen felt that Elmer Lach of the Canadiens was holding him. Instead of waiting for a whistle to see whether I thought so or not, Allen started arguing with me, and Elmer put the puck in the Chicago net. The Black Hawks fans went wild, tossing debris all over the ice. It must have been 20 minutes before they stopped throwing things at us.

I had Ed Mepham and Jim Primeau as my linesmen and we stood in the center of the ice to avoid the litter. Finally, I sent Primeau over to the bench saying, "Get Dutton in the corner there and ask him what the hell I should do."

Primeau came back to me about five minutes later. He reported Red's answer: "You got yourself into it, now get yourself out of it!" That didn't help me very much, and from then on I had to have a police escort into, as well as out of, the Chicago rink. Still, in all those years only one fan actually hit me; that was in Boston during a Stanley Cup series between the Bruins and the Toronto Maple Leafs.

I had refereed a game in Montreal the night before and had to come down through New York in order to get to Boston the next day. When I arrived at the train station in New York I picked up a paper and noticed front page pictures of the Boston players with cuts and bruises all over their faces. That made up my mind how I was going to referee the next game in Boston.

There was only one thing to do: crack down early in the game with penalties. As it turned out I called 17 penalties in the first period alone, five of them against Wild Bill Ezinicki. After his fifth penalty, Ezinicki said to me, "Bill, what are you doing? What the hell are you doing?"

"What would you do if you were in my position?" I asked.

"I'd do the same thing," he said.

But in the second period the rough stuff continued, although not as bad. During one play there was a scramble along the side of the ice and I tried to avoid the action by hoisting myself up on the sideboards. Just as I did, some fan who'd rolled up his newspaper like a club hit me over the head with it. He hit me so hard I was knocked out cold.

Then a funny thing happened. Earlier in the game I had given Jimmy Thomson, the Toronto defenseman, a misconduct penalty, which carried an automatic fine. Thomson had come back on the ice just before I got hit on the head and when I regained my senses he skated over to me and pointed toward the seats. "Bill," he said, "there's the guy who hit you." I had the guy thrown out of the rink and the incident proved what I knew all along: players may disagree with the referee but they don't want fans interfering with their game. As for the fan, I got a letter from him a week later apologizing.

I was never hit by a player. The closest I ever came to that was in a game between the Leafs and Red Wings in Detroit. I had my finger pointed at Tod Sloan of the Leafs, ready to give him a delayed penalty. Before I blew the whistle he skated by and called me something other than my proper name. I said, "That's it. Misconduct!" After I blew the whistle I called, "Ten and two," and when he heard that he came storming out with his hand raised as if to strike me. I gave him a game misconduct penalty but he never did hit me.

That was small potatoes, however, compared to some of the trouble I saw. Once, I was handling a game between the Red Wings and Canadiens at the Forum in the early 1940s. That was when Detroit had a pretty good club, with guys like Don Grosso, Sid Abel, Eddie Wares, and Jimmy Orlando and Jack Stewart on defense. Orlando was a Montreal boy and his family always came out to see Detroit play the Canadiens.

We were in the second period of the game when a fight broke out in the stands. Orlando looked up and realized that his father was in the middle of it. So he climbs over the boards and starts up the steps in the stands with skates, stick, and all, and the rest of the Detroit team follows him before I could stop them. The last guy I could get to was Eddie Wares, who was going up there with his stick in his hand. I yelled, "Eddie, drop your stick! Drop your stick!" He dropped it all right, but somebody hit him right on top of the head with a bottle and cut him wide open. I was sorry I had told him to drop the stick, and to make matters worse, I had to ride down to New York that night on the same bus with the Red Wings. It was murder.

At least an incident like that stopped the action on the ice and gave me a little rest. There were some games where I was really exhausted at the end. In fact, I refereed the longest game ever handled with one official. It went into sudden-death overtime and didn't end until 1:30 in the morning. When it was over my legs were so swollen I could hardly take my skates off and my ankles remained puffed up for several days after. But it didn't stop me from officiating my next turn. As a matter of fact, I never missed an assignment in my 16 years in the NHL.

The longer I refereed the easier it became. When I started refereeing I travelled all alone, and when I'd come to a city I'd work with a hometown linesman. And, as much as I don't like to use the word *homer*, there was such a thing in those days. Then Campbell came along and changed things. Hometown linesmen were eliminated and replaced by linesmen who traveled around the league just like referees. But that wasn't all he did to make a referee's life more pleasant. Previously, when a referee called a penalty, he was sure to have 10 people around him arguing; Campbell changed that so only the captain or alternate captain could discuss the penalty. Then the circle was added around the penalty timekeeper's area to prevent players from interfering with the referee when he announced his penalty.

I was the one responsible for developing all the arm signals now used in the NHL. I started using them from almost the first day I was in the league but they were only made official the year after I retired.

This was all because I studied the game; before each one I'd examine the recent history of the two teams so I knew what to expect from them. Sometimes I'd phone the referee who handled the teams a day or two earlier to get his impressions. If I felt my game was going to be especially rough I'd get the two centers out for the opening faceoff and caution them, "This is going to be a tough one. Be careful."

Of course, silly things happen. Once during a game between the Black Hawks and Americans, Red Dutton, manager of the Americans, complained that Chicago's goalie Sam LoPresti was wearing pads that were too wide. The rule book says the pads cannot be wider than 10 inches. "I want you to measure LoPresti's pads," said Dutton.

So I went out and measured his pads and they were 10¼" wide. Dutton yelled, "See, see, I told you he was over the limit. We're goin' to protest!"

Then Paul Thompson, the Black Hawks coach, said, very lethargically, "Bill, measure Robinson's pads." Robinson was the Americans goalie; his pads were 10½" wide.

Another funny thing took place in Chicago when Johnny Mariucci was on defense for the Black Hawks. In the early 1940s in Chicago Stadium, the gallery gods had a habit of playing cards before the game started. Once the action began these fans would wrap up their deck of cards with a rubber band and keep them handy just in case they didn't like the referee's decision.

Midway in the game I gave Mariucci a misconduct penalty and suddenly all those damn cards flew out of the balcony onto the ice. Meanwhile, Mariucci kept giving me the business from the penalty box.

I leaned over, picked up a bunch of cards, skated to the penalty box, and handed them to Mariucci. "John," I said, "you're gonna be here awhile. You might as well play."

Jack Adams of Detroit gave me the toughest time of anybody, but I don't think I'm unique in saying this. He'd constantly put pressure on the referees and try to intimidate them by continual needling. I don't know if it really worked; I imagine it might have with some of the guys.

On the other hand, there were the milder, pleasant types like Frank Boucher, who managed and coached the Rangers for so long. Boucher was always out to advance the game. Frank Selke, the manager of the Canadiens, was also like that.

If there was one thing I really objected to over the years, it was the idea introduced by Toronto of taking films of the game and then, a day or two later, asking the league to look at them to pick out the referee's mistakes. It's very easy to referee on Sunday a game played on Saturday.

Detroit also gave me trouble; when the Red Wings had that powerhouse hockey club in the early 1950s, they'd needle me like crazy. They had the best team in the league for five or six years and they'd let you know it in more ways than one. But if I said anything back to them, it was apt to wind up in the NHL office.

When I look back on all those years in the NHL I know I'd do it all over again the same way. Hockey's been great to me and I hope I've contributed as much to it. That's an old phrase but it's true.

Why, I would even find myself yelling at the referees sometimes. But I never called the referee a "blind bat" because I knew I might only be half right saying it.

Part II
The Post–World War II Years

Chuck Rayner
The Rangers' First
Hall of Fame Goalie

BORN: Sutherland, Saskatchewan, August 11, 1920

DIED: October 6, 2002

POSITION: Goalie, New York Americans, 1940–41; Brooklyn Americans, 1941–42; New York Rangers, 1945–53

AWARDS/HONORS: Hart Memorial Trophy, 1950; NHL Second Team All-Star, 1949–51; NHL All-Star Game, 1949–52; Hockey Hall of Fame, 1973

He was originally a member of the New York Americans, but by the time Chuck Rayner got there they had been renamed the Brooklyn Americans.

World War II was upon us, and like so many NHLers, Rayner enlisted in the Canadian Armed Forces where he remained until hostilities ended and he returned to New York. Unfortunately there were no New York Americans left. The team had been disbanded and players such as Rayner were allotted to the six remaining NHL teams. And that's how "Bonnie Prince Charlie" became a Ranger.

As it happened the Blueshirts also had their prewar goalie back, which meant that coach Frank Boucher had both Rayner and Sugar Jim Henry.

Rayner eventually won the starting job and became one of the most beloved athletes in New York City history.

I met Chuck late in his career after he had taken the team to Game 7 of the Stanley Cup Finals in 1950, losing in double overtime to Detroit. He also won the Hart Trophy despite playing for a fourth-place team.

I got friendly with Rayner the following year when the Rangers Fan Club was organized, and we remained in touch well after his retirement.

The sad part of Charlie's career was that he never had a strong supporting cast, but being the affable fellow that he was, he was just happy to play hockey. He remains one of my all-time favorite Rangers.

We were in New York one night playing the Leafs, and it was getting late in the game. I don't even remember if we were winning or losing; all of a sudden the puck was on my stick. I took a couple of strides toward the blue line and fired the puck down the ice. I'm not sure I would have skated the puck down, even if I could, but they had that rule prohibiting goalies from crossing the red line. Anyway, I shot the puck down, and it pretty nearly went in. Missed by about two or three inches, and don't you think [Toronto goalie Turk] Broda was surprised?

Those were the days when there was only one goalie on the team. There was no such thing as a two-goalie system. If a guy got hurt in goal during the game, he tried his best to stay in there. The teams didn't even carry a second goalie. If the visiting team's goalie got hurt and couldn't continue, then the home team had to supply a backup.

It was great at first. Jim Henry and I both enjoyed it. We didn't switch off games, we switched off shifts. About every third or fourth line change, we would change. It was all right in the beginning, but it became a problem later. I would be in goal and just get warmed up when there'd be a line change and I'd come off. Then Sugar Jim got in there, and by the time he'd warmed up, out he'd come.

I had to finally pack it in after the 1952–53 season. I had damaged the cartilage in my knee, pulled it out of shape. The doctor told me to get it operated on, which I did. And it held up for a while. Then the knee started to weaken, finally to the point where I didn't think I could do the job anymore.

I got hit in the right jaw one night in Chicago, broke it. The next night I got hit in the left jaw. Didn't break it, but I might as well have. During the

Goalie Chuck Rayner at Iceland, the Rangers' practice facility above the old Madison Square Garden.

game it didn't usually hurt so much; your hurts didn't feel so bad when your body was hot. It was after the game, when you cooled off, then it was bad.

There's no doubt the mask had added a lot to the goalie's game. I know at first the fellas were a little reluctant to put it on, but you can see how much good the things have done in the long run.

I wasn't fond of coaching for a few reasons. The decisions you had to make sometimes I didn't like at all. I didn't like having to tell a kid he was being traded. If he had a family, he'd have to pack them up, too. I didn't like having to break that kind of news to a kid. But I did like being around the kids.

I don't know about that slap shot they use in today's game. I'm not sure whether it's good or bad for the game. I'm certainly glad I didn't have to face it. I faced "Boom Boom" Geoffrion a few times, but he hadn't really perfected the thing yet. Thank God.

I think the World Hockey Association was a good idea, but it didn't really work out. When there were only six teams you had to produce or else. Now with all the teams you have more bargaining power. The money's much different, too. When I played my first year in New York I was paid around $9,000. That was big money then.

chapter two

Camille Henry
The Skinniest Ranger

BORN: Quebec City, Quebec, January 31, 1933

DIED: September 11, 1997

POSITION: Center, New York Rangers, 1953–65; Chicago Black Hawks, 1964–65; St. Louis Blues, 1968–70

AWARDS/HONORS: Calder Memorial Trophy, 1954; Lady Byng Memorial Trophy, 1958; NHL Second Team All-Star, 1958; NHL All-Star Game, 1958, 1963–64

They didn't call him "The Eel" for nothing. As slippery as any Rangers forward, Camille Henry was almost too skinny to survive in the NHL. But somehow he managed by employing a combination of smarts and skills when it came to putting pucks where they belonged.

Once I went to work for the Rangers, Camille and I became close buddies and we had some memorable times. One that I remember in particular was a trip to an elementary school in the Bronx. During the evenings I was studying for my master's degree in education, and one of my professors, Robert Petluck, liked to have athletes talk to his kids. Although Cammy was not getting paid a penny for the appearance, he readily accepted and wowed the kids (it also helped me get an A in my education class).

We stayed close right through Henry's coaching stint with the New York Raiders of the World Hockey Association, which was an abysmal failure because his players took unfair advantage of Cammy's good nature.

Eventually he moved back to Canada, hit bad times, and died at a very young age, virtually forgotten for his Rangers heroics.

I was a Montreal fan growing up. Like most kids growing up in Quebec I wanted to be just like Maurice "The Rocket" Richard, but right from the start they said I was too small, that I'd never make the National Hockey League. Even in Bantam. But the two years I played there I led the league in scoring. Then in Midget, when I was 14, I hardly made the team. But those two years I led that league in scoring. When I was 16 I moved up to Juvenile, and I led the league that year, too. They kept saying I was too small.

[Phil Watson] was a great hockey coach, maybe the best I ever had in my whole career. But he didn't know how to talk to his players. He didn't know how to treat men like men. He had a complex about not speaking the English language perfectly. He also thought that there was a clique of players on the Rangers who were against him. He thought Bill Gadsby was the leader, accused him of leading a rebellion against him. Watson thought I was in the clique along with Andy Hebenton, Andy Bathgate, and Gump Worsley. There were about six of us, according to Phil. I think he thought the whole world was against him.

I remember just before he got fired we were in Montreal. We had our usual noon meeting to talk about the game and get in a light skate. I was the first one out on the ice. Phil Watson came right over to me and started getting on my butt. He said the only reason I was in the National Hockey League was because of him. That I was no damn good, too small, couldn't play defense. This all started about 12:00, and at 2:30 he was still going strong.

Finally Muzz Patrick, who was the general manager at the time, came in and said, "Phil, that's enough. The players have to get their rest." On the way out Watson walked over to Eddie Shack and asked him if the day's lecture had done him any good. Eddie the Entertainer pointed at his left ear and said, "In one ear, out the other."

All the guys on the team were really great to me; they accepted me right off the bat. The only thing was when everybody would be making jokes in the locker room, it would take me a little while to translate and figure out what the joke was. I couldn't come back like I wanted to because it would always be too late.

Camille Henry was the first pointman to be used on a power play.

In Quebec City most of the players were French, except Aggie Kukulowicz. He stayed at my house and late at night we would be in the bedroom and he would speak French to me and I would answer him in English. Now Aggie's a Russian interpreter. I guess he had a good ear for languages.

Mr. Boucher called me when we were breaking camp—I thought he was going to tell me he was sending me down to the minor league team—and he said to me, "Cammy, I think you can make the National Hockey League. I have my 20 players right now, but I would like to carry you with the team because I think you can learn a lot just from watching."

The season started in Detroit and I didn't dress. In the second period Dean Prentice dislocated his shoulder, giving me my chance. The next night we were in Chicago and Boucher told me to dress. We won 5–3. I scored a goal and got an assist.

Max Bentley was the biggest help I ever had in hockey for one simple reason: he talked hockey with me nonstop. If I wanted to stay up all night talking about how to play certain guys and what to do in certain types of situations, Max would stay up with me. When we went on road trips and had those long train rides, he used to have to kick me out of his room at 5:00 in the morning. That's all we would do, talk hockey.

He was also a very exciting player to watch. I remember one night we were in Detroit, and Max told me he was going to score a goal against them, and this was when they had guys like Howe, Lindsay, Delvecchio, Red Kelly, and Sawchuk in net. So I told him if he was going to score one, I was going to score one, too.

In the second period we had a power play and Max was on the ice. He took the puck on his stick and skated all the way down the ice through Howe, Lindsay, Kelly, and Bob Goldham, and then put a move on Terry Sawchuk and scored a goal. He skated over to the bench and winked. I said, "Don't forget about me," and he said, "Don't worry, you'll score."

We were out on the ice about a minute later when Max got the puck again. He started a mad dash toward the Detroit goal, right through their defense, just like the first time. He got right in front of Sawchuk, pulled him out, and had him cold turkey, but instead of shooting he passed the puck over to where I had come down on the left side. There was no way in the world I could have missed, so I put the puck in the net just that easy. That's what kind of guy Max Bentley was.

I think the trade [that sent Henry to Chicago in 1965] was made simply because my back was sore. I had my third bad spasm at training camp and the doctor told me if I wanted to continue my career I would have to have it operated on at the end of the season, and that I could play that season only if I wore a special brace to protect the vertebrae, which were beginning to rub together.

I went to see Mr. Ivan and Mr. Reay as soon as we got back because I wanted to tell them about my back problem. They welcomed me and told me they just wanted me to help them win the Stanley Cup. We talked for a while and eventually I got around to the subject of my back. I told them I needed an operation. They told me not to worry, just play, everything would be fine.

They finally asked me to go and see their doctor to determine whether or not I really needed the operation. I said fine, and I went to see him. He took all the X-rays and told me to my face that if I were his brother, and with the back I had, he would tell me not to have the operation.

The phone rang in the doctor's office and it was Dr. Yana in New York. All I could hear was the doctor on my end saying, "Yes, I understand. Yes, I see. Yes, I agree. Thank you very much." And he hung up, turned to me, and—after 45 minutes of trying to convince me I didn't need the operation—told me to go to New York and have the operation.

Billy Reay told me I'd be better off playing in the Central League to get back in top condition. I could see the writing on the wall. I decided to pack my bags and go home, take some time to think things out.

[In Kansas City] I had to be carried to the bench, but I couldn't leave because I still had to coach the team. I could feel the knee start swelling up, and I knew right there and then that there was no way I was going to play hockey again. I still wanted to play, but I knew I couldn't.

When I came back with the Raiders, I was really taking what I thought would be a shortcut back to the Rangers organization. I figured if I did a good job with the Raiders, the Rangers would take notice and I could get a job with them.

The first two years after I left the Raiders all I wanted to do was hide. I was heartbroken. I never had the talent some of those guys had. I certainly never made the money they were making, but I loved the game, and they didn't seem to give a damn.

chapter three

Cal Gardner
Instigator of the
Biggest Rangers Fight

BORN: Transcona, Manitoba, October 30, 1924

DIED: October 10, 2001

POSITION: Center, New York Rangers, 1945–48; Toronto Maple Leafs, 1948–52; Chicago Black Hawks, 1952–53; Boston Bruins, 1953–57

AWARDS/HONORS: NHL All-Star Game, 1948–49

A Rangers hero who eventually came back to haunt them as a Bruin, Cal Gardner was a product of the Blueshirts farm system.

Back in the 1940s, the Rangers sponsored a Junior team in Winnipeg, Manitoba. It was called the Winnipeg Rangers and from that franchise numerous potential stars graduated to New York.

However, they didn't go directly to the Blueshirts because the first stop was invariably the New York Rovers, who played Sunday afternoon games at the old Madison Square Garden.

Gardner was one of those Rovers who eventually graduated to the big club, only he did it in a unique way.

Cal and his linemates, Rene Trudell and Church Russell, comprised what was called "The Atomic Line," which steamrolled over opposition in the Eastern loop. The line was so good that Rangers manager Frank Boucher promoted them to the Blueshirts as a unit.

That was the good news. The bad news was that only Gardner excelled and proved to be one of the best young Rangers until he became the centerpiece of a pivotal trade to Toronto.

As a Ranger, Cal was involved with several notable episodes. Easily the one that gained him the most notoriety involved an on-ice riot that exploded on the night of March 16, 1947, at the old Madison Square Garden.

Battling Montreal for the final playoff berth, the Rangers trailed 4–3 late in the game. At that point, Gardner severely injured Canadiens defenseman Ken Reardon. This precipitated what many believed to be the biggest fight in NHL history.

Gardner survived the battle, but was traded to Toronto for the start of the 1948–49 season in what was a major deal that brought the Rangers ace defenseman Wally Stanowski.

Years later, Gardner would wind up with the Bruins, and, this time, severely damaged the Rangers' playoff chances in yet another bizarre episode.

These stories were related to me by Cal many years after he had retired and was broadcasting in Toronto. You'll find some of these yarns in Gardner's words below.

Like so many Canadian kids, I started playing on an outdoor rink prior to World War II. The Great Depression was still on and life was tough in those days. When the war started I joined the Canadian Navy and once it was over I tried to get into pro hockey. In those days the Rangers were very big in my home province. For years they had training camp at the old Winnipeg Arena and they had a top Juniors level club called the Winnipeg Rangers. Those were the days before the draft when each of the six NHL clubs ran their own Junior teams.

I must have impressed the brass because they assigned me to the New York Rovers, which was quite a big deal in a lot of ways. First of all, it meant that I'd be playing out of Madison Square Garden, and secondly, the Rovers played in the old Eastern League, which was only two steps away from the NHL. Chances were good that if I impressed the Rangers who were in charge—mostly the boss, Frank Boucher—I might someday make it all the way to the big club. Little did I realize the manner in which I'd skip a big rung on the hockey ladder.

What happened was this: when I tried out for the Rovers—as a center—in 1945, a guy from my hometown, Transcona, Manitoba, by the name of Rene

Trudell was there. He was a left wing and Church Russell, from Winnipeg, was there, too. Originally our line was to be rounded out by Gus Schwartz on the left side, but he got hurt so they put Rene in his place. Russell, Trudell, and I clicked immediately and we started the 1945–46 season as the top line with the Rovers.

Remember, this was right after World War II had ended and everybody had the atomic bomb on their minds because it was dropped on Hiroshima the previous summer. With that in mind some newspaperman named us "The Atomic Line" and the nickname stuck. One reason for that happened to be that we turned out to be one of the best lines in the entire Eastern League. The Rovers were drawing big crowds—up to 15,000 sometimes—to the Sunday afternoon games at the Garden, and we kept getting more and more ink.

Ironically, our big break came because our parent team, the Rangers, was struggling for the fourth straight season and manager Frank Boucher felt he had to do something to help his club. As far as I know, what he did was unprecedented; instead of promoting me, or Rene, or Church, our entire line was moved right up to the Rangers. It was late in the season so we only got into about 16 or so games, but still, the Atomic Line going from the Eastern League to The Show in one leap was big stuff.

Boucher kept our line together and we played the entire 1946–47 season as a unit, and that gave management enough time to decide what to do with us because the original novelty of the promotion had long ago worn off. What happened was that Russell—who looked so good as a Rover—just couldn't cut it in the NHL and it had a lot to do with the fact that the game was rougher up there and Church got a bit "puck-shy." Or, as they like to say when a player doesn't want to get hurt, "Russell started to throw a little snow." He eventually got dropped in the 1947–48 season and wound up in the minors. He was a good guy and a good hockey player but he got a little scared of the body contact and that cut his Rangers career short. The deal was that you either could play at the NHL level or you were gone, so Church was gone. Meanwhile, I stayed with the Rangers as did Rene but he was about seven years older than I and that was against him. In those days NHL owners regarded anyone over the age of 30 as over the hill.

Unlike his two linemates, Gardner developed into a hard-nosed center with more than passing scoring ability. Tall and wiry, he enjoyed the rough style of play prevalent in the post-war era. During his second NHL season, 1946–47, the Rangers were making their first serious bid for a playoff berth since the spring of 1942. The Blueshirts ran neck and neck with the Montreal Canadiens for the fourth and final playoff berth in the six-team league. Finally the clubs met head-on the evening of March 16, 1947, with the winner virtually guaranteed entry into the postseason playoffs.

It was a viciously played contest with Montreal leading 4–3 when a collision led to a melee, which erupted into what many historians consider the biggest fight in hockey history. The chief protagonists were Gardner and Ken Reardon, a future Hall of Fame defenseman who also happened to be one of the toughest players of all time. Trouble began immediately after Reardon carried the puck toward center ice when Bryan Hextall of the Rangers attempted a hip check. Reardon bounced off the Rangers right wing right into Gardner's waiting stick. "My upper lip," said Reardon, "felt as if it had been sawed off my face."

Reardon was helped off the ice—right past the Rangers bench—prompting a fan to needle the Montrealer. Reardon swung his stick at the fan and then a cop grabbed the Canadien, who soon was ushered to the Garden infirmary. When Reardon tried to hit the fan, a number of Rangers got off the bench to check out the fracas. From the opposite side of the ice, Montreal coach Dick Irvin thought that the Rangers were going to attack his player. He yelled, "Get the hell over there" to his troops and what ensued was every player on each team—goalies included—slugging it out. So crazy was the Pier Six brawl that a call was put out to the New York City Police Riot Squad, and eventually cops brought peace to the ice.

Amazingly, Reardon did not realize who had hit him and would not learn that it was Gardner until long after the brawl had taken place. When Reardon did learn that Cal had cut him, a blood feud between the players erupted that ended only when NHL president Clarence Campbell intervened. Here's how Gardner remembered his running battle with Reardon, starting with the clash itself on Garden ice.

This was such an important game for us because the fans were desperate for the Rangers to make the playoffs. Montreal had a terrific team during the war and won the Stanley Cup again in 1946, but this time they were struggling just to

Cal Gardner was part of one of hockey's all-time biggest brawls during a game against the Montreal Canadiens in 1947. (NY Rangers Archive)

get in and they had us by the ropes with a one-goal lead late in the game. Dick Irvin, their coach, may have believed that I deliberately high-sticked Reardon, but that wasn't the case. As he came at me I tried to sidestep him and when I did the blade of my stick caught his lip, cutting him pretty bad. To tell you the truth, I didn't even know who he was until after it happened. Hey, I was still only a rookie in the NHL at the time.

As a matter of fact, I didn't even think much about Reardon after the brawl was over since we lost the game and missed the playoffs again. But hell would break loose later on. Hal Laycoe, a defenseman and my teammate on the Rangers when the incident with Reardon happened, got traded to Montreal. Once Laycoe settled in with his new teammates he told Reardon that I was the one who cut him up so badly.

Meanwhile, the Maple Leafs were on their way to becoming the first NHL dynasty [three straight Stanley Cups] after winning championships in 1947 and 1948. They had three of the best centers of all time: Syl Apps, Ted Kennedy, and Max Bentley. But after the 1948 Cup win, Apps stunned the team by announcing his retirement. This was a real stunner since Apps was captain when Toronto won the Cup in 1942, as well as 1947 and 1948. Conn Smythe, who ran the Leafs, was desperate to become the first manager to have a team that won three Cups in a row but he had to replace Apps to do so and that's where I came into the picture.

Smythe decided that of all the centers in the NHL, I was the one he wanted most of all, and he swung a deal with Boucher that sent me to the Maple Leafs. By that time Reardon was after me and made no secret about it, either. At the time *Sport* magazine was the number one monthly that covered all major teams on the continent and that's where Reardon went to publicize our feud. In the *Sport* article Ken said he would break my jaw. Soon after the article hit the stands we played Montreal and we had a real nasty stick-swinging affair, but this one also was strange because Reardon was going after one of my teammates, Bill Ezinicki. He swung his stick at Ezzie, missed him, and hit me. So I retaliated right back with my stick and then we got into a fist fight.

I wound up getting fined $250 and Reardon only $200 and I'm not sure why. By that time every one in the league was aware of the Gardner-Reardon feud and a season later we took it up a notch. I made the mistake of dropping my head to look at the puck and the next thing I knew Reardon caught me with an elbow. It was bad stuff and I wound up with a double compound fracture of the jaw. I must have been in the hospital for eight or nine weeks recovering. But I came back and played the rest of the year.

By now NHL president Clarence Campbell decided that he would do something about me and Ken, and his decision was interesting to say the least. Campbell made Reardon put up a $1,000 bond to be forfeited to the league if he deliberately attempted to injure me again. And all the fuss goes back to that collision we had when I was a Ranger.

After leaving New York, Gardner played on Stanley Cup winners in 1949 and 1951 with Toronto but in June of 1953 he was sold to the Boston Bruins. Playing for the Beantowners, Gardner once again would be involved in the Rangers' fate, only this time in a reverse—and perverse—way.

The Blueshirts had reached the playoffs in the 1947–48 season and again in 1949–50 but then another drought set in. The New Yorkers would miss the postseason in 1951, 1952, and 1953. But during the 1953–54 season Frank Boucher had crafted a relatively competitive squad that depended in large part on former Leaf—and Gardner's teammate and roommate in Toronto—Max Bentley. Because of their prior relationship, Gardner was able to talk the Rangers out of a playoff berth.

This may seem preposterous but you will understand after my explanation, which begins with the un-retiring of Bentley, who had previously starred for the Chicago Black Hawks and Maple Leafs. After Bentley had proven to Boucher that he still had the goods, the Rangers boss then talked Max's older brother, Doug, out of retirement in January of 1954. The Bentleys spurred New York into a fierce battle for the playoffs with the Boston Bruins.

When the teams met for the last time at Boston Garden, it was assumed that the victor would gain the final spot for a postseason run. Knowing that Max Bentley was key to the Rangers' success—especially on the power play—the former Blueshirts center employed a unique strategy to—in a sense—talk the Rangers out of a playoff berth. Here's how Cal described it to me in his own words.

Since Max and I had become good friends when we were teammates in Toronto, I got to know him really well. For better or worse, I learned that he was a first-class hypochondriac and likely got worse about his "illnesses" as he got older. Well, by the time he joined the Rangers his hypochondria was as bad as it ever was, although he managed to play through it and do well in New York, especially after his brother, Doug, joined the team in midseason.

As much as I loved Max as a pal and a player, when we met in the fateful game in March 1954, I also was thinking about my team, the Bruins, and how much we wanted to finish fourth. That's when I decided to work on Max's hypochondria and the worries he had about his health. So when we skated on the ice for the pregame warmup, I made it a point to say something to him every time we skated past each other on the ice. My comments were offhanded but also right to the point.

I started off by saying, "Max, you're not looking well," and then I worked on him from there. Next time we passed, I added, "What the devil are you doing on the ice?" And he began worrying more. The third time, I added, "Maxie, you look like you have a temperature of 102. You're not going to help the Rangers tonight!" Just to be sure, I repeated that warning when we came out for the opening faceoff.

It was apparent to me that Max was thinking about what I had told him. Being the nervous wreck that he was, he must have been thinking about it all game. This much I can guarantee: we won the hockey game and made the playoffs. Bentley was awful that night, which is why I liked to think that I "talked" the Rangers out of the playoffs.

Jack McCartan

From the Olympics
to the Blueshirts

BORN: St. Paul, Minnesota, August 5, 1935

POSITION: Goalie, New York Rangers, 1959–61

AWARDS/HONORS: United States Hockey Hall of Fame, 1983

When Jack McCartan became a Ranger after the 1960 gold medal win at Squaw Valley, I was not pleased.

One of my heroes, Al Rollins, was making a comeback in goal for the Blueshirts and deserved to remain the starting goalie.

But the Rangers brass felt they could cash in on McCartan's Olympic glory— which they did—and Rollins became a forgotten man.

To his credit, McCartan played very well in his first few games as a Ranger, particularly after he stoned Gordie Howe on a breakaway in his New York debut.

However, I never believed that McCartan was as good as his Olympic notices, and wrote just that in The Hockey News. *Although that didn't endear me to the goalie, McCartan and I remained on speaking terms, even after the Rangers finally demoted him the following season.*

Still, Jack's short stint between the pipes remains one of the truly outstanding events in Rangers annals. In retrospect it is amazing that McCartan accomplished as much as he had in hockey.

Goalie Jack McCartan won gold as a member of the U.S. Olympic hockey team in 1960 and was enshrined as a member of the United States Hockey Hall of Fame in 1983. (NY Rangers Archive)

Actually, baseball was my number one sport as a kid growing up in Minnesota. I think that if I had concentrated only on baseball from the very beginning I could have made it as a professional, but a lot of things intervened, including college. As a matter of fact, I didn't even pursue a career in baseball, as a third baseman, until I graduated from Minnesota. Meanwhile, I was playing a lot of hockey. I started skating on outdoor rinks. We weren't very organized in those days right after World War II and we didn't play many games. To see an NHL game was a big deal. As a matter of fact, until I actually played in an NHL game I hadn't seen more than five in my whole life. We didn't have television and there was no NHL around Minnesota then. The only time I saw games was when Minnesota would be in Chicago and we'd catch a Black Hawks game. Brother, was I in awe of the NHL.

When McCartan made the 1960 U.S. Olympic team, not much was expected of him and his teammates. "We were definitely underdogs," said his coach, Jack Riley. "We couldn't possibly win a gold medal. At least that's what they all said before we hit the ice."

McCartan made 39 saves, most of them difficult, and allowed only one goal in the team's 2–1 victory over Canada. "He made one incredible save after another," said Riley. On Saturday, February 27, the Americans faced off against the Soviet team. More than 10,000 spectators jammed Blyth Arena for the contest while millions watched the game on television. The Americans won the game 3–2, then beat Czechoslovakia 9–4 to claim gold.

For us, it was a special feeling because something like that had never happened before or since.

The reason why I was able to get a chance with the Rangers was because of all the publicity. The ratio between the publicity and my possibilities of actually making it to the NHL was about 80 percent publicity and 20 percent fact. But the Rangers made me the offer—the thrill of my life—and naturally I accepted. All in all I would say that I had some fair success and at other times it was very hard. The NHL was a good league at the time. I was up against players like Bobby Hull, Gordie Howe, Alex Delvecchio, and all the great Montreal players.

I didn't last all that long but I wouldn't have changed a thing. I was happy enough just to get to the NHL, to compete, to see what it was like. I always loved the game of hockey, love it today and always will.

I just happened to get hot at the right time. Anyone can get hot and things just went my way. I played that whole year [1960] with the Olympic team and the Rangers and I lost only one game—that was the second-to-last home game of the year at Madison Square Garden against the Bruins. If the Rangers had played every game the way they played when I was in the nets they would have been a playoff club, not fifth or sixth. Maybe they played well for me because they were afraid of getting blown right out of town.

Come to think of it, I didn't have that much of a career but getting a chance to play in the NHL made it all worthwhile.

On October 19, 1960, Chicago's Reggie Fleming engaged in a famous brawl with the Rangers. Fleming set the record for most penalty minutes in a game.

It started with a fight between Fleming and Eddie Shack of our club. Shack was cooling off after they broke it up and he skated to center ice. Fleming picked up a stick and started up to center ice after Shack. Well, I didn't know about the guy and thought he was going to hatchet Shack with his stick. So I slid my stick up toward center ice so Shack could pick it up and defend himself.

Well, nothing happened up there so I skated up to get my stick back. It just so happened that Fleming was skating back to pick up his gloves behind the net. As we passed, he suckered me with a punch to the head. That was it, and I had all I could do to stay on my feet. He hit me with a good shot and I saw stars.

I always was fairly competitive, but I never overdid it. But I could get hot and let my temper take over. I never would want to hit anyone with my stick. I think the only time I ever swung at anyone was when I was with St. Louis of the Central League and we were playing Omaha, a farm club of the Canadiens. There were a lot of good-but-cocky players on that club and they liked to shoot the puck at the goalie's head. On this one night they were shooting it at my head and I told one of them, "Do that again and I'm going to hit you right over the head with my stick." It's the only time I ever tried to hit a guy, but, of course, I never did. I just swung my stick at him.

I was playing in the Western League when I stopped one of Andy Bathgate's blasts with my nose. After that I said enough is enough and began wearing the mask. Once I put it on I began to wonder how a goalie like Glenn Hall could have played 500 straight games without ever putting on a mask.

I was pretty well finished by then but I enjoyed playing in Minnesota. All things considered it was a good break for me.

chapter five

Max Bentley
The Dipsy Doodle Dandy
From Delisle

BORN: Delisle, Saskatchewan, March 1, 1920

DIED: January 19, 1984

POSITION: Center, Chicago Black Hawks, 1940–43, 1945–47; Toronto Maple Leafs, 1947–53; New York Rangers, 1953–54

AWARDS/HONORS: Lady Byng Memorial Trophy, 1943; Hart Memorial Trophy, 1946; NHL All-Star, 1946; NHL Second Team All-Star, 1947; NHL All-Star Game, 1947–49, 1951; Hockey Hall of Fame, 1966

One of the most electrifying players ever to skate in big-league hockey, Max Bentley owned the nifty nickname to go with his style. The Saskatchewan-born center was called "The Dipsy Doodle Dandy from Delisle."

Before coming to the Rangers, Bentley starred on the Chicago Black Hawks Pony Line along with his older brother Doug and Bill Mosienko. In one of the biggest trades of all time, Max was dispatched to Toronto in November of 1947, whereupon he won Stanley Cups in 1948, 1949, and 1951.

By the 1952–53 season, Max's play had slipped and he eventually wound up with the Rangers for the 1953–54 season.

Maxy had been my hero when he was in Toronto and even more so in the twilight of his career as a Ranger. My dear friend Ira Gitler from the Rangers Fan

Club remembers skating with Bentley at the Iceland rink atop the old Garden on Eighth Avenue between 49th and 50th streets.

My most vivid recollection of Maxy actually was off ice. At the end of the 1953–54 season, the hockey writers of New York combined with the Fan Club to hold a dinner-dance at the Martinique Hotel off Herald Square.

Maxy had a big grin on his face all night. He seemed to be appreciating the fact that he had a glorious half-season skating with big brother Doug, who was also happy as a lark.

It was the last hurrah for both Bentleys but an unforgettable one for me.

Our whole life was hockey, right from the start. That's all we did. If [Doug and I] weren't at school, we were at the rink [built in 1917 by his dad] or playing shinny out in the road. That's where we learned to stickhandle, playing in the road. Then we'd get to the rink and play with the bigger boys and their older brothers and get beat up a little bit. We'd go home crying and then come right back again. We loved it. The Rangers stars, Bill and Bun Cook, were Doug's and my favorite players. They came from right near us in Saskatchewan and we idolized them.

Max's wrist shot worked in Junior hockey, in intermediate hockey, and, finally, professional hockey, when he skated for Providence in the fast American League.

Going down to Providence was a wonderful coincidence. Who do you think my coach was? None other than Bun Cook, the man who I had idolized. He was a terrific man and I couldn't believe my good fortune.

[Being traded from Chicago] was really rough. I had played with Doug all my life and I didn't really have to go, but the Black Hawks were getting five players and I thought the trade might strengthen them. I went to a good team but I never got to play with two players like Doug and Mosienko [again].

That club was the best. We finished first and beat Detroit, a real good club, in the Finals in four straight games. Our goaltender, Turk Broda, was the best, and I say that from experience because I shot at him for years.

"I never thought [Black Hawks president Bill] Tobin would ever part with him," said Conn Smythe. "When I was in Chicago, I talked about Max to the waitresses

Hall of Famer Max Bentley, the "Dipsy Doodle Dandy from Delisle."

at the hotel, the clerk at his desk, the taxi driver, and many others, and they all said the same thing: that Tobin wouldn't trade Max. He was too popular."

[Smythe] was a terrific man. All he asked was that you try; and if you didn't try you wouldn't last in Toronto. I thought the world of him; he was like a dad to me. He loved his hockey and knew it well. Same with our coach, Hap Day. It got to be great to play on that team. There was discipline; no fooling around. In Chicago we couldn't get much ice to practice. In Toronto we practiced every day when we didn't play.

To me, [Maurice] Richard was the most dangerous scorer I've ever seen. Every time he was on the ice I was scared to death. If he got the puck inside the blue line he was dynamite. I've seen him carry two defensemen on his back and still manage to score.

As a player I was never booed. I felt that if I couldn't do my job properly, I'd get out of the game. Nobody was going to boo me.

Frank [Boucher] was a very good friend of Doug's and mine. He asked me to sign with the Rangers and I told him I wasn't up to par—that I could play in, maybe, half the games and my back was really bothering me. I didn't really want to go to New York but Frank offered me a good contract and since he was a good guy I said I'd go back for a year. Before I ever signed I kept telling Frank that I wasn't my old self but he seemed to be willing to use me part-time on the power play and whatnot, so I did it. But it wasn't much fun since my back had become a big problem. Every night after a game I'd go home and be crazy with pain.

The good part was the Rangers' decision to talk Doug into a comeback and have him rejoin me on a line with Edgar Laprade, another grand old playmaker who also was making a comeback with the Rangers. When Doug flew in to New York from Saskatoon the players went wild with stories. That night we were playing the Bruins and Doug was dog-tired; he had had almost no sleep at all during the trip and we were all wondering how he'd be able to skate with all the wear and tear of traveling and his age and the fact that we were playing a team that was neck-and-neck with us for a playoff berth.

Madison Square Garden was packed that night and we gave the fans quite a show. I centered Doug, and Laprade, even though he normally was a center, played on the wing. Once we got started it was just like old times, and Edgar fit in perfectly with us. The Bruins went ahead but Doug came back and scored our first goal and it ignited our team. Our line had a field day against the Boston goalie, Jim Henry. We beat the Bruins by a big score and the place went crazy.

I felt that if we could have made the playoffs we would have been a lot of trouble for the opposition. I felt our team was really coming on at the end.

In April 1979, my former coach in Toronto, Hap Day, said in an article that I was the most exciting player he ever saw. And that made me feel good. Of course when I was playing I would never think about that. I wouldn't think about it anymore than I did when Doug and I were kids and we would shoot the puck and stickhandle on the veranda of our house in Delisle. We just did it and that's how we learned.

I'd do it all over again for nothing. But I sure would like to get some of the money the boys are getting today. My first salary with Chicago was $2,500 a year. After I led the league in scoring two years in a row I got a raise up to $10,000. In Toronto, Conn Smythe paid me $16,500 and then he raised me to $18,000. I was happy with the little bit of money I did make and I invested it in land. I had some very nice property that ran right up to Delisle.

I had my picture taken with Pat O'Brien, Ann Rutherford, and Mickey Rooney. Ann Rutherford had her arms around my neck when we posed. Then there was another with Lana Turner, who was called "The Sweater Girl" in those days. It was all very exciting.

You may remember Barbara Ann Scott, the great Canadian figure skating champion of the late 1940s. Well, one night we were playing in Boston Garden and I had one of the best games I ever played in my life. After it was over she stopped me and said, "I've never seen anything like you," and we took a picture together.

[My son] Lynn was probably the best hockey player I ever saw for his age. When he started playing Junior hockey in Saskatoon at age 16 he was 6'1", a beautiful skater and a big man. Everybody said he was a better stickhandler than I was. But he fell in love when he was very young and got married and just didn't want to play anymore. When Lynn was still 16 I took him to Toronto to see Conn Smythe and Conn wanted him to stay but Lynn wouldn't. He was in love with a girl in the West and they eventually got married.

[My second son] Gary was a pretty good hockey player and he wanted to be one but he wasn't good enough to go all the way. For a while I had my heart set on seeing both of them turn pro but neither one did, and that set me back for a while.

Today, I don't see players going down the ice and coming up to an opponent and saying, "Here it is!" and then the puck isn't there anymore and the guy is around the defenseman ready for a shot on goal. In my day there were lots of players who could do that.

We never used the slap shot. It was the wrist shot and the backhand all the time. That's why I like the Russians; they get their shots away quickly and they pass beautifully and make great plays. That's the type of game we would play when I was in the six-team NHL!

chapter six

Andy Bathgate
The Best Post-War Right Wing

BORN: Winnipeg, Manitoba, August 28, 1932

POSITION: Right Wing, New York Rangers, 1952–64; Toronto Maple Leafs, 1963–65; Detroit Red Wings, 1965–67; Pittsburgh Penguins, 1967–68, 1970–71; Vancouver Canucks [WHL], 1968–70; Vancouver Blazers [WHA], 1974

AWARDS/HONORS: Hart Memorial Trophy, 1959; NHL First Team All-Star, 1959, 1962; NHL Second Team All-Star, 1958, 1963; NHL All-Star Game 1957–64; Hockey Hall of Fame, 1978

Following World War II, the Rangers established a Junior hockey team in the Ontario city of Guelph, not far from Toronto. It was called the Biltmore Mad Hatters, thanks to the Biltmore Hat Company, which was one of Guelph's biggest industries.

By the start of the 1950s, the Biltmores became the dominant Junior team in Canada.

Thanks to such teenage stars as Dean Prentice, Harry Howell, Lou Fontinato, and Ron Murphy, the Biltmores were the talk of Canada and each of those players would eventually graduate to the Rangers.

By far the best of the crop was Andy Bathgate, a right wing with a thunderous shot and ready fists if ever challenged to a fight.

I got to know Andy shortly after he was promoted to New York and we became good friends in the 1954–55 season when I worked for the club. Gentlemanly and affable, Andy went on to become a Hall of Famer although he never won a Cup in New York. He had that distinction after being traded to the Maple Leafs.

Over the years I've seen Andy on his various trips to the Garden and he remains one of the most majestic Rangers of all time.

My father deserves all the credit for getting me started in hockey. He started the first community center in Winnipeg and was very active working with kids. He would flood the outdoor rink so that we could play, and we played and played and played. With the war on and people pretty poor where we came from, hockey was the cheapest thing, so we played hockey as much as possible. We never did anything else during the winter. For seven months we just played hockey.

It was a rough time for us. There was just me, my mother, and an older sister living in Winnipeg, so we all moved to Guelph. When we got there I made the Junior A team [the Mad Hatters] and my brother Frank and I were teammates. He was in his last year of Junior and I was a rookie. We had a good year and won the Ontario Hockey Association championship. From then on it kept getting better.

The Rangers took the three of us to New York but I was the one who didn't make it, at first. On Christmas Eve they shipped me to Vancouver while Dean Prentice and Harry Howell stayed with the Rangers. I stayed in Vancouver that year and part of the next year. The Rangers had me back for 20 games in 1953–54 and I got my first two NHL goals. But this time they shipped me out to Cleveland of the American League. I did well with the Barons and, finally, I was called back to New York.

It was the beginning of an 11-year stay in New York and it had its ups and downs, or should I say downs and ups, because when we were starting in around 1953 and 1954 the team was pretty down. We were drawing crowds as low as 5,000 a game. It was so bad at times that they would give away little orchids for the ladies and try all sorts of gimmicks. There was at least one game when the entire balcony was closed because the crowd was so small and the fans were all seated below in the arena. At that time it was considered a great thing if you could get 8,000 or 9,000 people in the building for one of our games. But then we started winning in 1955–56 and the crowds started to pick up. Still, it wasn't easy for us. We were small-town Canadians coming to the big city and we felt lost and scared. We were even frightened to get a writeup on the sports pages of the New York papers. Although everyone knew us in Canada, we could move around New York City and go unnoticed. I remember going to banquets with a lot of players from other sports and getting that message hit home to me.

There was a time when I was sitting on a dais with Frank Gifford and Alex Webster, who were stars with the football Giants, and the fans recognized them as easily as they would the President of the United States. Me, they didn't know. But the more we won, the more the recognition started to come and the Rangers got respectable.

When I got to New York, we had a small team. All the centermen, for example, were 150- to 160-pounders. We were little and young; a lot of us had just turned 20. But the nucleus was there and with Guelph turning out a lot of players it wouldn't have taken too long for the Rangers to be a contender. After our group there was another with guys like Rod Gilbert, Jean Ratelle, and Eddie Shack coming up. But management made a mistake; instead of keeping all the Guelph kids, they began to trade. In 1964, when they traded me to Toronto, the club was on the right track. But I was disappointed that, while I played for New York, we never finished first or won the Stanley Cup.

I worked on my shooting at least 15 minutes every single day. To my mind shooting practice is one of the most overlooked aspects of the game. I see coaches emphasizing skating all the time, but to me, the most important thing is shooting the puck. When you shoot the puck it's not how straight it is that counts, it's the quickness of the release, and that's what I kept working on when I was a Ranger.

In a way it was difficult practicing a shot in New York. We never worked out on Madison Square Garden ice. What we did was hold our scrimmages in a rink called Iceland, which was located on the top floor of the Garden and was used as a regular public skating rink and also by figure skating clubs. There were two things wrong with Iceland: first, it wasn't a standard-size rink, it was smaller. And, second, it had aluminum sideboards. That meant that when you took a shot off the boards the noise was worse than in a boiler factory. It was positively deafening. And with me shooting and shooting off the aluminum boards some of the fellows on our team got a little upset with me. In between shots, I would reach in my pocket where I carried a spring and I kept my hands working so that they got as strong as possible.

Right wing Andy Bathgate, whose No. 9 jersey was retired in 2009.

In my entire life I've never had a drink or a cigarette, and it made me feel good as a player. Some nights I'd go out on the ice and I'd know just by looking at the opposition that I was in much better shape than them and it was to my advantage, both physically and mentally.

The fact that I was partly responsible for getting the Rangers players to join the [players] association didn't endear me to management and I began to hear rumblings that I would be traded. The animosity of the front office didn't surprise me. I knew that Doug Harvey, who had been a star with the Canadiens, was traded from Montreal, and Ted Lindsay, who was one of the best of the Red Wings, had been traded from Detroit because of their involvement with the union.

It was a strange situation at the time because the Rangers were considering all kinds of trades. They had this young center, Jean Ratelle, who had a great future, and I had heard they were planning to trade him, too. I said at the time that they shouldn't trade Ratelle because he had a great future. Next thing I knew, I was traded.

I wasn't all that disappointed. After all, I had played my best years in New York but we still didn't come near winning the Stanley Cup. I could see that the Rangers weren't building enough in that direction. I loved playing in New York, make no mistake about that, but I also wanted to play for a Cup winner before I hung up my skates. When I got to Toronto I immediately discovered that the fans resented the trade. They liked Dick Duff, Bob Nevin, and they saw a future in the kids, Arnie Brown and Rod Seiling. But I got hot in the playoffs, scored two winning goals, and we won the Cup. The Finals were some series. Detroit had us down three games to two but we won the sixth game and the seventh and final game was in Toronto. I scored a goal in the first period to put us ahead 1–0, and it stayed that way until the middle of the third period when we broke it open and won 4–0.

My feelings after we won the Cup were interesting. No question that it was nice, but there was something missing, and it was the fact that I had been brought up a Ranger, all the way from Junior hockey. Meanwhile, the majority of the Toronto players had been developed in the Maple Leafs Junior system, so I was something of an outsider. Even worse, I was an outsider who had taken the place of guys on the Leafs who were pretty close friends of those who still were with the club.

In fact, the whole environment in Toronto was different from New York. With the Maple Leafs, all the players had their friends and families living close by, so when they left the rink they all went their own way. In New York, the hockey players formed their own tight little community. After a game we would all stick together, chum together. For the six-month period that we were in New York we did this almost continually. The companionship in New York was something special and I wasn't really prepared for the change when I got to Toronto.

Frankly, I didn't enjoy Punch [Imlach]'s methods of training. By my second season in Toronto I just wasn't enjoying playing so I spoke to Punch and I had to give him a reason to get me out of Toronto. So I said something to one of the reporters; Punch overemphasized it and I wound up in Detroit.

Maybe Punch thought I was lazy but I think training had to be fun. When a practice gets to be too much, the player becomes mentally fatigued and he doesn't want to play. You lose your enthusiasm and that's what happened to me under Imlach. So I didn't mind going to Detroit. I became a teammate of Gordie Howe and Alex Delvecchio and a bunch of good guys. For a while, they tried me on a line with Delvecchio centering and Howe on the right. To accommodate them, I worked on the left wing but I couldn't make the adjustment. Gordie and I seemed to be on collision course all the time.

Now, we were in the Finals against the Canadiens. The first two games were in Montreal and we won them both at the Forum. I thought we had the Cup in the bag as we returned to Detroit for the next two games.

I don't know what happened to us. We had a good hockey club but once Montreal won that first game it was unbelievable, like a nightmare.

I still say we should have won the Cup, but at least I had been on a Cup winner before. One of our defensemen, Bill Gadsby, had been in the NHL for 20 years and never played for a Stanley Cup team. Imagine how he must have felt.

I was still enjoying the game. When I wasn't playing hockey I worked on my golf in the summer and had a driving range in Toronto. When Pittsburgh drafted me [in the Expansion Draft] I had no intention of quitting. Heck, I was still enjoying the game and, in my first year with the Penguins, I wound up the highest scorer on all six expansion teams.

After that good first year with Pittsburgh I was enthused and looked forward to another season. The management told me, "Just do what you did last year, come to training camp, and take it easy." So, I came to camp and, what do you know, on the third day of camp they told me I'd been traded to Montreal. The Canadiens wanted me to go into coaching. No way; I had made my mind up that I wanted to play that year, and I was upset by the way the whole business was handled. When it comes to retirement the player likes to make the decision himself, or at least be given a little warning. Instead of quitting, I phoned a friend of mine in Vancouver and wound up playing for the Vancouver Canucks of the old Western League, and I had two of the most enjoyable years I've ever had in hockey. We were averaging about 12,000 fans per game and in the playoffs we packed the arena. I worked as hard in Vancouver as I ever worked in the NHL. Of all things, before the start of the 1970–71 season, the Penguins called me up again and I spent my last year in Pittsburgh.

I didn't enjoy that year at all. They didn't give me much ice time and I felt that I wanted to end my career somewhere where I could possibly buy an interest in the hockey club. I had a deal worked out but the Penguins wouldn't release me, and I was a little upset about that. All I remember is that I had six games to go to reach the 350-goal mark and I never got on the ice again. That was enough to tell me that the time had come. I decided to hang up my skates.

I played in the Swiss League in 1971. Considering that we only played a 22-game schedule, it was the most money I ever made in hockey. The Swiss-style game had a lot less body contact but not a lot less hitting. I had never seen so many people cut with sticks. You're not allowed to fight in the Swiss League. If you drop your gloves, you're out, automatically suspended. The Swiss skate like mad and play, mostly, on outdoor rinks. The town that I coached in had a population of only about 300 but for a couple of our games more than 9,000 fans showed up. What they would do is stand on the side of a mountain or wherever they could to get a glimpse of the rink. My family enjoyed the entire experience. We all took up skiing and my two kids became so good at it they'd rather ski than skate or anything.

When I joined the Vancouver Blazers in 1974, Joe Crozier ran the team, and I was brought in as assistant coach and manager. I wasn't in the best of shape because of an accident at home when I was building my kids a rink.

I had bought some new lumber and was putting some points on the end to support the boards and I hit a piece of wood. The nail split in two and went right through my eyeball. The accident left me with only 20-percent vision in my right eye. Still, Crozier, who was having problems with the Blazers, asked me to put the skates on for a couple of games. At first I tried to wear a helmet with a mask but after two games I discarded that. Played 11 games in all. Of those the club won about seven and Crozier wanted me to continue playing. But he was only willing to pay me the same money I was getting as an assistant coach and I felt it was too much of a risk, so I decided to hang them up.

Part III
The Boys of Expansion

chapter one

Glenn Healy
Backup to the Cup

BORN: Pickering, Ontario, August 23, 1962

POSITION: Goalie, Los Angeles Kings, 1986–89; New York Islanders, 1989–93; New York Rangers, 1993–97; Toronto Maple Leafs, 1997–2001

One of the funniest fellows of any era of hockey, Glenn Healy emerged on the New York scene as a member of the Islanders. He was a much better goalie than many expected and was heroic when Al Arbour's sextet upset the Stanley Cup champion Penguins in the 1992–93 playoffs.

Since I worked all the Islander broadcasts in those days, I came to appreciate Healy's artistry in goal and jokes in the dressing room. Glenn and teammate Patrick Flatley formed a comedy team, which was featured on SportsChannel's Heals and Flats Show, *which became a regular on the network.*

To the dismay of Islanders fans, Healy signed on with the Rangers for the 1993–94 season and was backup to Mike Richter as Mike Keenan's club went on to win the Rangers' first Stanley Cup in 54 years.

During the summer of 1989, I went to Ireland on vacation with my buddy, Pat Flatley. Once we got there, Pat phoned home to get the names of his relatives he was supposed to visit in Ireland.

Pat was talking to his mother and she said, "Glenn is now a member of the New York Rangers."

Goalie Glenn Healy, shown here with teammate Esa Tikkanen, was Mike Richter's backup on the 1993–94 Stanley Cup champions.

Winding up on the other side of the East River was the last place I figured would be my destination. The Rangers and Islanders were such keen rivals that they never traded with each other. I told Pat to have his mother read the story to him line by line, and then he explained that the transaction was a bit more complicated and I actually was a "member" of the Anaheim Mighty Ducks and Tampa Bay Lightning before the Rangers acquired me. The truth is, I didn't find out the true nuances of what happened until I got back home.

What happened was that [Islanders general manager] Don Maloney chose not to protect me in the Expansion Draft. If I had been picked up by the Ducks or stayed in Tampa I absolutely would have been thrilled and would have played as hard as I would have anywhere. But I was very fortunate that

[Rangers general manager] Neil Smith got his clutches on me and gave me a chance to win a Stanley Cup.

That was quite a thrill, but then again, the first NHL game I ever played in Los Angeles is a night I will cherish as well. In that sense, there definitely was a sense of satisfaction that my hard, painstaking work, starting with ball hockey in the driveway, paid off. It makes one think back to the games played in bitter cold outdoors and running those extra miles to keep in shape. All of those elements contributed to the big event, which was playing in the NHL.

When I went between the pipes for the first time with L.A. all of those memories came to the fore and I felt as if I was being rewarded for all the time I had put in.

The night I'd like to forget? Hmmm. The way I look at it, we're in the NHL for a very short period of time in our lives, and while we're at the top, we're doing something we love and getting paid very well to boot. How many people can say that about their jobs?

As a result, my philosophy was to enjoy every moment I was in the NHL because I knew it could be taken away from me so quickly. It seems that overnight age can catch up to you and the next thing you know, you're working a regular job. I don't think there ever was a night when I wished that I was doing something else because I've enjoyed every NHL day and night that I've had.

My wife, Susie, was very supportive of me in every sense of the word. I don't think an athlete can play this game without having someone who is very supportive and at your side.

In our jobs, as players we have teammates who really are our "family," so to speak. On the other hand, wives find themselves thrust into the hockey situations when their husbands get traded. Then they have to stay behind and clean up the mess and get the kids off to school, or out of a school and into a new school.

Our rewards as players are great, although the psychological side can be like a roller coaster. Our highs are very high and our lows are very low, although ideally we would like to stay on an even keel. The problem is, when the club is mired in a losing streak, it's tough to keep your chin up, and when you're on a winning streak, it's tough keeping your head out of the clouds.

Hockey wives are the ones who keep your head up when it's down and down when it's too far up. They are the family stabilizers.

Going to the Rangers was a very positive event in my life. Players with that organization get tremendous support from management. Their facilities are second to none and one of the most enjoyable parts has been the emphasis on winning the Stanley Cup.

When I got the Cup ring it meant so much, especially the fact that the Healy name went on the mug. That signifies all the times my folks got up at 5:00 in the morning to get me to practice, and it signifies the times when my sister sacrificed her time to come and watch my games, and it stands for all those who helped me succeed and achieve that goal. The ring is important to the players personally but to have my family's name on the Cup means more to me than anything else.

The difference between playing on the Island and for the Rangers was my role with the respective teams. With the Rangers, Mike Richter was my team-mate in goal and I knew what his position was with the club. In 1995–96, when Mike got hurt, I was called on to play a lot of games and reporters began asking me about it being "a burden" on me.

That's the New York media. They like to blow things like that out of pro-portion. I looked at it as if I'm one player of 20 on this hockey club. Yeah, there was a lot written when Ricky was hurt and I had to play, but I chose to ignore it. I didn't look at my role as any more important than anyone else's role. We all worked together and tried to play together as a team so that at the end of the day we won games. We needed everybody to win games, not just Glenn Healy and not just Mark Messier. Everybody had to contribute.

My policy was to take it one game at a time. I put forth my best effort each time I was out there, and at the end of it, I could look at myself in the mirror and say that I'd done my best. My best means being prepared for the game and anything it took to win. I must be at my best for the game. When that game was over, I approached the next game the very same way.

When it was time to relax, as in the off-season, I liked to Sea-Doo and play golf. During the season I liked to play chess. When Nick Kypreos was still with the Rangers, I would play chess with him on the plane trips—and kick his ass all the time. After he left, I began teaching Adam Graves how to play, but made sure not to teach him all the top tricks.

chapter two

Alexei Kovalev
The Rapid Russian

BORN: Togliatti, USSR, February 24, 1973

POSITION: Right Wing, New York Rangers, 1992–98, 2003–04; Pittsburgh Penguins, 1998–2003, 2010–11; Montreal Canadiens, 2004–09; Ottawa Senators, 2009–11; Florida Panthers, 2012–13

AWARDS/HONORS: NHL Second Team All-Star, 2008; NHL All-Star Game, 2001, 2003, 2009

Imagine a saxophone-playing forward who also flies his own planes. That is Alexei Kovalev, the Ranger who paved the way for the Blueshirts for the 1994 "Battle of the Hudson" playoff series victory over the New Jersey Devils. Kovy was as much fun as he was a solid sniper and always was good for an interview with me, which of course, eternally endeared him to The Maven.

Coming to New York for the first time, I was really scared because I was by myself. I had a girlfriend—now she is my wife—then and she didn't come until four months later. I was alone for four months and didn't know any words of English, and I was scared to go outside and talk to the people. I was really scared when people would try to ask me something. I was like, "Wha…?"

Anyhow, I really had a good time with the team whether I knew any words or not, because everyone on the Rangers was trying to help me. When I would try to talk to them, I would use my fingers or arms. The one guy who helped me along was Sergei Nemchinov, my teammate on the Rangers, who also was Russian. He helped me a lot at the beginning. After that we met a lot more Russian guys around New York. They told me that I didn't have to be scared because I could speak a little English.

"If you don't know all the words," they said, "use your arms, anything. You will learn because people will try to help you."

Then I got a teacher to help me and she began coming to my house three times a week, and she did that right through the 1995–96 season.

During my first two years in New York, I would not take my lessons all the time that I should have taken them. When my teacher would call to set up a lesson, I would say, "I'm a little tired. When I come home after playing I want to take a nap."

My teacher didn't like that. She would say, "You have to work hard to learn English."

"Maybe next time," I would tell her. Frankly, I didn't work hard enough, but I knew that I just had to talk to people and they would appreciate what I was doing. When Euginia [Kovalev's wife] came over, it was a lot easier for me. Back home, she was a very active tennis player; she played three, four times a week. She used to play in the same stadium that I had played in when I was with Dynamo [in Moscow].

That's when I met her. When I would return from team practices, that was when she came back. She played tennis very well, but she never intended to become a pro. She played just for the fun of it and for herself. Then she decided to teach kids and had a really good time. I always would pick her up from her job.

It was a lot of trouble to bring Euginia to America. She had to get a visa from the embassy in Russia. My agent did a lot of work to bring her here. In the second year, the embassy did not want to give her a visa because she was still my girlfriend. They said, "You have to be married." So we decided to get married.

It took us maybe two hours to get married. We paid 150 bucks and got a certificate. We went right away to the American Embassy and got the visa the next day and flew to the United States. Now we can come and go to Russia together.

Alexei Kovalev broke into the NHL with the Rangers in 1992. (Bruce Bennett Studio/
NY Rangers)

When I finally came to North America, I started training with the Rangers. I remember playing our first game against the Islanders. Like in Russia, if the other team takes the puck in their zone, they can go all the way to the neutral zone and our zone. In the NHL there's a third guy behind just helping in the defensive zone. I saw the defensemen trying to use all the spots. When a guy takes the puck on the boards, the defenseman comes right away. They didn't give you a chance to make a pass or get away from the defensive zone.

Because the rinks in the NHL are smaller than those [Olympic-sized] rinks in Russia, I decided to stay in the neutral zone more and do as the other forwards and defensemen do. The trick—because of the rink size—was that you don't have to skate as much; you just had to be smarter.

Now I have reached my goal. When I played in Togliatti, my goal was to play in Moscow in a higher group. I learned something in Moscow, so I decided to go to the NHL. That was another jump.

Kovalev was part of several notable moments in Rangers history, including New York's epic playoff series with the New Jersey Devils in 1994. (Bruce Bennett Studio/ NY Rangers)

I now stay in America because I like it here. This life gave me a chance to help my parents. I wanted very much to bring my parents to New York because they had not been anywhere before. I wanted to show them what kind of life it is in the United States.

When they finally came here, they were really excited. My father said, "Alexei, now I don't have to worry about you. You know what you're doing."

But I still remember when I was young, and I always asked my parents for money to go to the park and play computer games. Every time I asked for my money, my mom or dad would say, "How many times do you want to go there and play games?" And I would say, "You don't want to give me the money, or what? When I play at a higher [pro] level of hockey, I'll give you back your money."

They were laughing about that and they kept saying, "You did it. We're so proud of you."

I told them, "My career is my life. I'm not going to be a guy working outside not knowing what he's going to do. I found what I want and I'm happy." Now I have my own life. I have my house, my cars, and everything. I'm not worried that I won't be able to support my parents.

Often, I think of what my father went through. He worked in a car factory for 30 years, and they never gave him a car. When I came home I said, "Forget about the factory, they'll never give you a car." Then I bought him a new car.

He was crying that I did it for him.

It's funny. During the NHL lockout in 1994–95, I went to Togliatti and played for my team and they gave me a car. That was like my present for my father's birthday.

Even though we played in Manhattan, I lived in a suburb called Mamaroneck in Westchester County [north of the city]. A lot of people ask me, "How do you like living in New York City?" I say I don't like living in the city because it's too crowded and too noisy.

I came into Manhattan a lot of times and I've stayed in hotels in Manhattan, but there are a lot of trucks and a lot of noise. Sometimes, when I'm not playing hockey, I visit New York City to go out or just walk around and see the different sights and sometimes to see my friend, Igor, to take saxophone lessons.

In Russia, I played it for a while when I was eight to 10 years old, but there was a problem—it was very hard to find a saxophone over there. And then you have to find a teacher. I forgot the sax for a while, but after I came to New York, I think it was Sergei Nemchinov's wife who told me about a sax player who sometimes worked out with the players.

One day, I met him and asked if he wanted to teach me how to play sax. "That's always been my dream—to play that instrument," I told him.

He agreed. He lives in New York City and sometimes I would go to his apartment for lessons. It was exciting for me to play that instrument, but Igor didn't have a lot of time because he was traveling a lot so on my own time, I started learning the notes. I love music, both listening and playing, and I especially liked the sax because so many people play the piano but so few played this instrument.

But hockey was still number one, and winning the Stanley Cup in 1994 with the Rangers was very special. I always say winning one is not enough, and it doesn't mean you have to stop playing hockey. You have to think about winning it again. Players like Mark Messier have won a lot of Stanley Cups, and I wanted to do the same thing.

It was important to me to be a leader on the Rangers and a star. Sitting on the bench was not for me. I wanted to be the kind of player who was a leader in the playoffs, where people would say about me, "Oh, this guy Kovalev really helped the Rangers win the Stanley Cup."

Every year was different, just like every NHL team's style is different. I noticed that the Canadian teams have learned from the Russians. Then you have the changes in coaches. One coach likes to make a lot of combinations while other coaches like a simpler style, just hard skating and shooting.

Myself, I tried to do creative things that would make the fans happy. Once I passed the puck to myself behind my back. That kind of thing made the fans wake up.

Hockey writers have questioned which position is best for me, center or wing. At center, I played a more improvising type of game because I had more control of the puck. Everything starts from the center. When I played center, there was a lot of work. I had to play defense, support my wings, and play the offensive neutral zone. But I liked a lot of work. The year we won the Stanley Cup, I played center with Steve Larmer and Stephane Matteau; we had a really good time.

Kovalev scored 430 regular season goals in his NHL career, including 142 for the Rangers. (Bruce Bennett Studio/NY Rangers)

I liked carrying the puck. Sometimes I was 100 percent sure that I could bring the puck all the way to the offensive zone. When I played the point on the power play, I did a lot with the puck. I did it because I knew that I could do it, so I did it!

One of my best times was when we played New Jersey in the 1994 playoffs. The Devils were leading the series, three games to two, and we were at their rink for Game 6. Mike Keenan was coaching us that year, and we were losing the game 2–0 in the middle of the second period. I was so scared and I was looking at everybody and all the guys had their heads down. They didn't know what they were going to do.

I kept thinking that we had played 84 games in the regular season and had done so well and had won two playoff rounds already, and now everything was stopping so fast. I didn't want them to beat us so easily.

Then late in the second period, I felt that I could start to do it by myself. I knew that I could change the game. I had to do something and I did. I got the puck to the right side in the New Jersey zone. I faked a shot, then went in a little more and beat Martin Brodeur.

That enabled us to enter the third period down by only one goal and not two. Then we tied the score and went ahead to win. You must remember that was the night Mark Messier predicted that we would win the game. After that we won Game 7 in double overtime and beat Vancouver in the Finals.

It was a tough job to play hockey, and sometimes a lot of yelling goes on both among the players and coaches. The coach yelled to make us play harder, and the players yelled for various reasons. For instance, when I played with Steve Larmer, he was always yelling at me when I would lose a faceoff. But it was not like he was yelling to get me upset; he was just trying to help me.

I found out from my father and from my coaches that there always is something to learn in hockey. I hoped to learn as much as possible so that I could play to the best of my abilities.

chapter three

Brian Leetch
The Best of the Backliners

BORN: Corpus Christi, Texas, March 3, 1968

POSITION: Defenseman, New York Rangers, 1988–2004; Toronto Maple Leafs, 2004; Boston Bruins, 2005–06

AWARDS/HONORS: Calder Memorial Trophy, 1989; James Norris Memorial Trophy, 1992, 1997; Conn Smythe Trophy, 1994; NHL First Team All-Rookie, 1989; NHL First Team All-Star, 1992, 1997; NHL Second Team All-Star, 1991, 1994, 1996; NHL All-Star Game, 1990–92, 1994, 1996–98, 2001–02; Hockey Hall of Fame, 2009

Perhaps the greatest tribute to Connecticut's gift to the Rangers was that Brian Leetch survived an enormous buildup to eventually earn induction into the Hockey Hall of Fame. Leetch's level of excellence was so consistently high that he rarely suffered a letdown.

Although I was doing the rival Devils telecasts, when the "Battle of the Hudson" was at its most intense, Leetch was always a gracious and insightful interview for me.

Ironically over the past few years we have been colleagues working as hockey analysts for the Madison Square Garden Network.

I grew up in Cheshire, Connecticut, where my dad was the first manager of the Cheshire Skating Center. The rink opened when I was around five-and-a-half or six years old.

My neighborhood was full of young kids so we all did everything together, be it street hockey or kick ball. We would all go to the rink and play in the [hockey] clinics together. They had one regular-sized rink and one smaller-sized rink for the clinics.

One of the coaches happened to be my father, and he helped us to learn the game. Then we graduated up to the big rink and right on up through Mites, Squirts, Pee Wees, and Bantams. Usually we played weekend games, traveling around Connecticut and the New England area.

After practices, we always played street hockey. In those days, we didn't have the opportunity to see a great deal of hockey live, but we tried to play it whether it was on the ice or in the street every chance we had.

Without a doubt, my father was the biggest influence on my career. He was the coach or assistant coach for many of my teams. He was transportation to all the games. On the rides to and from the games, we would talk about hockey.

Away from the ice, he was also the biggest influence in my life, along with my mother, in the way they raised me. They taught me how to be a responsible individual and to respect my elders. It all comes from having a solid foundation at home, and I was lucky to have had that. I believe that was probably the most important thing in my youth: having both parents around to help me into maturity.

In addition to hockey, I also played quite a bit of baseball. I played up to my high school years and did well pitching because I could throw hard. But I never thought about taking baseball any further than that. The way I see it, there are so many people playing baseball, so many kids, that if you're a pitcher, your whole career is dependent on your arm, and that can go at any time.

Besides, my friendships were involved in hockey as opposed to baseball. Plus, I enjoyed hockey from a team aspect so that is a big reason why I stayed with hockey and went to college.

There was no question that I wanted to go to college. There was nothing that I thought of doing otherwise. I had hoped that if my hockey continued to improve there was a chance I could get a college scholarship and save my parents some money.

On the way up, I went to prep school [Avon Old Farms] for two years to try and help both my academics and athletics. I wanted to stay in New England so I could be close to home. I had some friends at Boston College, where my

Defenseman Brian Leetch's jersey hangs from Madison Square Garden's rafters.

dad had gone, but my dad wanted me to look at some other schools. I looked at New Hampshire, Providence, and Boston University, but I really wanted to go to Boston College, and it turned out to be a great decision for me.

As a freshman player, I was saddled with an initiation rite of having to sing a song on the bus. I played 37 games for BC that year and had nine goals and 38 assists. After one season with Boston College, I made it to the U.S. national team and then the Olympic team [1987–88]. I have a lot of thoughts about those days.

To begin with there were eight months of traveling on the road because we never had a home base. The great thing was that we had 25 guys who were all within three or four years of each other in age, and we were all college kids and enjoying ourselves to the max. It was the first time we had a little money in our pockets and the first time we were able to just play hockey and not have to worry about schoolwork or anything else for that matter. In a sense, it was a grind but we didn't realize how much of a grind until we got to the Olympics in Calgary.

After the Olympics, I came to the Rangers at the tail end of the 1987–88 season. That was the year we were neck and neck for a playoff berth and the Devils beat us out on the final night of the season.

We played the Devils in New Jersey near the end, and I had a fight with Pat Verbeek who was with the Devils at the time. You can go back and check the records and you will see that it is tough to find many fights that I was involved in, but on that night it was a very highly charged, emotional game. Tempers get short sometimes and things get a bit wild.

Even though I haven't fought much, I recognize that fighting has its place in a rough, physical, knock-down sport such as hockey. It is very fast and highly emotional, and sometimes the emotions get out of hand. But this is not to say that after the game such a fight remains a sore point. What takes place on the ice stays on the ice.

If you expect me to say that because of what happened years ago in that game that Verbeek and I are not friends, then you are sadly mistaken. I'm not the only one who had a fight with a guy and then, years later, found myself a teammate with him. It happens all the time.

From time to time, I have been asked by writers to make a direct comparison between myself and the legendary Bobby Orr. I've told newspapermen that that's ridiculous. I doubt that there will ever be another defenseman who comes along like Bobby who can change the game and be the dominant player in the game that Orr was. There were other great players before Orr and after Orr, but nobody has been the same. In terms of the offensive part of my game, if I got the chance, I liked to shoot. But I always looked to pass if there was an opportunity. I liked to draw someone to me and set somebody else up. You don't score too many goals when the goaltender is looking at you.

Professionally, the best thing that happened to me was winning the Stanley Cup in 1994. Hockey-wise, it was a great satisfaction to achieve that and especially to be on the Rangers, a team that had not won the Cup for so long. And there had been all that talk about the Rangers' jinx and that they would never win it.

To be a part of that victory was a great feeling, but it is something you have to personally go through to understand it. You kind of lose it after it is gone a few weeks later because it is such a high and it is such a place that only allows you to reach it for such a short time, which is why I always strived to get back there, because I knew what a feeling it was.

Shortly after we got our Stanley Cup ring, I wore it, but after that, I gave it to my dad. He had meant so much to me both privately and in my career that I thought it fitting he should have my Stanley Cup ring. He has worn it quite often since then. It seems that you are far removed from it once you finally get it.

The best thing would be to get it the very next day after you win the Cup, but we know that it doesn't happen like that.

chapter four

James Patrick
Wise Man of the Blue Line

BORN: Winnipeg, Manitoba, June 14, 1963

POSITION: Defenseman, New York Rangers, 1984–93; Hartford Whalers, 1993–94; Calgary Flames, 1994–98; Buffalo Sabres, 1998–2004

Sometimes during the early segments of an athlete's career he can be overcome with overhype, even though the press agentry is not his fault. This was the misfortune that afflicted Jim Neilson and other potential Rangers stars who failed to live up to their advanced billing.

In a sense, this could have brought down James Patrick but it didn't. Although he never reached Hall of Fame status he proved to be an accomplished defenseman both in his own zone and on the attack.

I spent many a memorable moment with Patrick but one in particular stands out, and that was a playoff preview that SportsChannel did in a midtown Manhattan studio. It featured James and then-Rangers general manager Craig Patrick (no relation).

Because we had to wait almost an hour while a defective camera was repaired, there was plenty of time to talk hockey, and that's when I got to know Gentlemen Jim better than ever.

A nicer guy you will never find. Here's what he had to say.

Ever since I was a six year old, I wanted to play in the NHL. My dad [Steve Sr.] played pro football with the Winnipeg Blue Bombers, yet hockey was still number one for me. It pretty well was always hockey because I was a product of my environment, growing up in Winnipeg. It's cold for so long and there was a rink on every street corner. Every kid played and when it wasn't ice hockey, it was ball hockey at lunchtime. I would put on my skates after school, and after dinner I would play on the outdoor rinks. Then in the summer, I went to hockey school and played still more ball hockey.

I did play football for two years in grade nine and grade 10, and I loved that as well. My dad wanted my brother and me to have the opportunity to try for football. Unfortunately, football wasn't supported that well in Winnipeg. In the summer I'd play catch with a football for hours, just with the kids on the block.

Whereas kids today are playing with computers and Nintendos, we would make up games—medicine ball and bean ball—and start playing. That's the way things were in those days and the environment I came from. Add to that the very positive influence from my father, who has been the biggest influence in my life. I don't know of a more honest person than him. I know about his beginnings and that he worked for everything he got. He wasn't a very talented football player when he started, but he worked real hard at it. He got his education late and then he started an insurance–real estate business that he had. He lived by the codes of discipline and hard work. Those are the philosophies that he instilled in us, my brothers and sisters.

Ever since my brother, Steve, and I turned pro, [my father] related to us how fortunate we were to have the opportunity to play hockey for a living. He stressed support and an educational environment. He also encouraged me to take summer courses and finish my college degree.

Not everyone had his line of thinking. In fact, when I played minor hockey, the atmosphere was not all that great. What I mean is that it was taken far too seriously by some of the people involved. I remember when I was 13 years old, we had a team rule that said you had to be at the game an hour before faceoff.

On this night, I was picked up by another player's father. I waited at the door for a half an hour and we arrived at the rink 20 minutes before the game, and it took me five minutes to get dressed.

The coach wound up benching me and the player who picked me up. We were scratched for two periods. Now, I look back on that episode and it strikes me as ludicrous. It's a shame that hockey is made so serious for young kids.

They should have fun and enjoy it; enjoy the competition, enjoy the fun of being on the ice and competing. To me, what that coach did was take away from the real purpose of the game.

Despite all that, I gradually moved up the ranks until the 1980–81 season when I played Tier 2 level hockey in Prince Albert, Saskatchewan. I played there for a specific reason, namely that I planned to attend university. Otherwise, I would have tried for Tier 1. But in order to keep my college eligibility, I had to stay in Tier 2.

My team, Prince Albert Raiders, won the Centennial Cup championship in 1980–81, and I won the tournament's Most Valuable Player Award as well as the Canadian Tier 2 Player of the Year Award. I was still a teenager and at that point my dreams were, number one, to play for Canada in the Olympics, and, number two, to follow that by playing in the NHL. I honestly did not know I could get drafted until halfway through that year. The draft had lowered the age the year before and then again that year.

I was playing Tier 2, trying to decide what college to go to and trying to improve as a player. In a sense I was a typical high school kid, and then, all of a sudden, I was drafted by the Rangers [first choice, ninth overall] in the 1981 NHL Entry Draft. Still, even though I was drafted, I knew I was going to go to college for one or two or whatever number of years, and as excited as I was about being picked by the Rangers, I figured the NHL was still a ways away.

It was now time for college and I chose North Dakota where I started in a four-year business management program. I went for two years and got most of my general arts requirements. I was about halfway toward my college degree when I left.

While there, I played two seasons for North Dakota [1981–82, 1982–83]. In the first year, we won the NCAA championship and I was named WCHA Rookie of the Year. A year later, I was a finalist for the Hobey Baker Award. All in all my two years at North Dakota was what I call one of the best experiences. We had a really good hockey club, for starters, and then combining the athletics and the academics and the college social life, that was terrific. A lot of young players who go straight from Junior to the pros miss out on that, and they're rushed into adulthood so quickly. After those two years, I went to the Canadian Olympic team and, finally, the Rangers.

James Patrick spent 10 seasons as a member of the Rangers and later served as an assistant coach for the Buffalo Sabres. (AP Images)

I remember the first time I was at the practice rink in New York after the Olympics. The Rangers had lost a couple of games and I was told that the team was going to have a conditioning practice.

I had taken some time off after the Olympics and had not skated for about 10 days up until that workout. I stepped on the ice and knew then and there that all the Rangers were looking at me, which made me nervous. Nevertheless, I was anticipating that day and even now I still remember the details.

First, there was the normal hour practice—Herb Brooks was our coach— and then we went through conditioning for a good half-hour after that. I was dead tired as I went through the laps with the other defensemen. At one point, I was half the length of ice behind the other guys; that's how rusty my skating was at that moment. In retrospect, it was a humorous scene, although at the time it wasn't funny.

I was very nervous but I tried not to say anything. Ron Greschner, one of the veteran defensemen, and some of the guys would talk to me, and I knew they had read all the clippings about me. After all, there was a buildup and I felt, "Geez, I'm on a pedestal here and the spotlight is shining on me." It was definitely nerve-wracking.

When New York hired Mike Keenan as coach, I personally thought it might be the best thing for me and that Mike would push me to the next level. I came to training camp in Rye, New York, and there were a lot of defensemen—a lot of good, young defensemen.

Keenan benched me for the first part of the season. I mean, I hardly played. One time I played six games and saw only two or three shifts. But I'll say this, Mike was very up front and said that I had to play better in order to play. I told him that if I played more, I'd play better.

Certainly, I don't know if Keenan had a prior agenda with me, but I do think he wanted to make some changes and I was one of them, and that's how I wound up in Hartford.

I felt I needed a change. I thought I still had the skills to help a lot of teams, but Keenan had basically relegated me to the press box. Mike just didn't like my style of play. He was the type of coach who went with four defensemen a lot so even in the games I did play, I hardly saw any ice. It was definitely time for a change.

Part IV
The All-Time Most Popular Rangers

chapter one

Rod Gilbert
Mr. Ranger

BORN: Montreal, Quebec, July 1, 1941

POSITION: Right Wing, New York Rangers, 1960-78

AWARDS/HONORS: Bill Masterton Trophy, 1976; Lester Patrick Trophy, 1991; NHL All-Star, 1964–65, 1967, 1969, 1970, 1972, 1975, 1977; NHL First Team All-Star 1971–72; NHL Second Team All-Star, 1967–68; Hockey Hall of Fame, 1982

There is one—and only one—Mr. New York Ranger.

That's Hall of Famer Rod Gilbert, who, once he donned the red-white-and-blue shirt, never left the Big Apple and to this day remains a Manhattan resident; he lives just a slap shot away from Madison Square Garden.

Of all the post–World War II Rangers, none have so fervently dedicated their lives to the team—which he still serves—and New York City more than the French Canadian who became beloved on Broadway after leaving his native Montreal.

What's more, no Ranger endured and survived the physical torment of two broken backs to enjoy a career rivaled only by other legendary New York right wings such as Bill Cook, Bryan Hextall, and Andy Bathgate.

That Gilbert was able to prevail is a tribute to both his own perseverance and grim determination and the Rangers' obsessive conviction that he could become an exceptional hockey player. The fact that New Yorkers also were desperate for a scorer after Bathgate was traded to Toronto in February 1964 played an important part in the Rangers' investment in Gilbert.

Gilbert's first full season as a Ranger (1962–63) was unimpressive from an artistic viewpoint. He scored only 11 goals and 20 assists and trailed far behind Kent Douglas of Toronto in voting for the Rookie of the Year Award. But he did manage to play in all of the Rangers' 70 games despite his aching back—and it was still aching.

"Even though I had the operation," he said at the time, "it was necessary for me to wear a special back brace. Once I tried to play without the brace I found I got tired right away."

The brace was a huge white corset consisting of heavy fiber and leather draped over thin tongues of steel extending from Gilbert's chest to his hips. Trainer Frank Paice would tighten the vise for Rod before every game to a point where breathing would be almost impossible.

"It was necessary," says Rod, "for me to stand up on the bench during the rest just so I could catch my breath."

Back problems continued to afflict the promising scorer through the mid-1960s, and a second operation was performed in February 1966.

"At the time I had not yet tasted the glory of the NHL," he said. "Now I knew what it was like to be a big-leaguer. I knew what I would be missing if I didn't pull through.

"You know, you never miss what you never had. Once you have a taste, the personal satisfaction, you can say, well, I've done some good work.

"When I was 20, after the first operation, I hadn't experienced that feeling. I could have returned to school and gone into something else. But when I was 24, hockey was all I really loved to play and do. I wanted so desperately to come back.

"By the end of the first week I could see daylight. The pain began ebbing. My taste returned. The wave of good wishes inspired me. Slowly but surely, all good things began falling into place, and I realized I had acted wisely. Just as they promised, I was released from the hospital after three weeks and began the long period of recuperation.

"My instructions were clear: no golf, no strenuous activities, no automobile driving, just relaxation, much the same as after the first operation.

"After getting out of the hospital I visited Grossinger's resort hotel in the Catskill Mountains, northwest of New York City. After that I embarked on a summer cruise on the *Leonardo da Vinci* to the Caribbean. It was difficult for me to enjoy myself, although everybody else seemed to be having a good time.

"All I could think about was what it would be like when I stepped on the ice at training camp in September."

The news was good, and continued into the start of the season. On October 22, 1966, he scored three goals against Toronto, the first time he ever scored three goals in one NHL game. The second operation was so successful—or,

Hall of Famer Rod Gilbert holds team records for career goals (406) and points (1,021).

so it seemed—he glibly dismissed questions about his controversial back problems.

"What back?" he would reply. "I don't remember a thing about it. All the misery and agony faded into the background on the ice. Now I'm convinced it never happened. I never want to remember again."

Gilbert's road to the Hall of Fame was rapidly being paved by big games. In a contest at the Montreal Forum on February 24, 1968, Gilbert scored four goals against the Canadiens and fired 16 shots on goal, which at the time was an NHL record, and remains the most shots any Blueshirt has taken in a single contest.

During the semifinal round of the playoffs against the Chicago Black Hawks, Gilbert scored two goals within six seconds at Chicago Stadium. He finished the season in fifth place among scorers, with 29 goals and 48 assists for 77 points, and led the Rangers in playoff scoring with five goals in six games.

Gilbert and his boyhood chum and linemate Jean Ratelle were leading the Rangers offensively. The duo was soon bolstered by the addition of Vic Hadfield on left wing.

In 1971–72, this trio collected 139 goals and 312 points, making them the most productive unit in the NHL. Gilbert was the lowest point-producer on what came to be known as the GAG ("goal a game") Line, but his career high of 43 goals and 97 points earned him All-Star honors as the league's top right wing.

Gilbert was now in reach of the Rangers' club scoring records held by Andy Bathgate. Scoring what he termed a "routine goal," against the New York Islanders, Rod passed Bathgate's 272 career goals early in the 1973–74 campaign. He then set a new team point record by scoring two more goals against the Minnesota North Stars, giving him 730 points.

By the time Rod retired during the 1977–78 season, he owned several team records, including most seasons played (18), career goals (406), and career points (1,021). He is the only player with more than 400 goals and 1,000 points while sporting a Rangers uniform.

During his career, Gilbert set or equaled 20 Blueshirts team scoring records. Rod amassed 12 20-goal seasons, and when he retired, he was second only to Gordie Howe in NHL career points.

One of Broadway's most prolific scorers accomplished this with a blazing slap shot. Some in the media thought he should change his play by taking more wrist shots, but Gilbert and coach Emile Francis disagreed.

"If I told Rod not to slap the puck," recalled Francis. "It would have been like me telling Bobby Hull to stop slapping. It was a helluva weapon, the kind you didn't discourage an offensive player from using."

It was no surprise when Rod's No. 7 became the first of the club's sweaters to be retired. After all, he was a winner of the Bill Masterton Award, played for Canada at the 1977 World Championships, was a member of Team Canada at the Summit Series, and capped his impressive career by being inducted into the Hockey Hall of Fame in 1982.

As an added fillip, Rod was given the Lester Patrick Award in 1991 for outstanding service to hockey in America. Over the past few decades, he also has served as the Rangers' director of community relations.

Therefore, there can be absolutely no denying that this Man about Manhattan has earned the sobriquet Mr. Ranger!

chapter two

Mark Messier
The Cup Maker

BORN: Edmonton, Alberta, January 18, 1961

POSITION: Center, Edmonton Oilers, 1979–91; New York Rangers, 1991–97; Vancouver Canucks, 1997–2000; New York Rangers, 2000–04

AWARDS/HONORS: Conn Smythe Trophy, 1984; Hart Memorial Trophy, 1990, 1992; Ted Lindsay Award, 1990, 1992; NHL All-Star, 1982–83, 1990, 1992; NHL Second Team All-Star, 1984; NHL All-Star Game, 1982–84, 1986, 1988–92, 1994, 1996–98, 2000, 2004; Hockey Hall of Fame, 2007

Who is the all-time hockey king of New York?

Ask that question to any contemporary Rangers fan over the age of 20 and the answer inevitably would be either Rod Gilbert or Mark Messier.

The irony, of course, is that "Moose" became the Big Apple's hockey messiah despite the fact that he made a name for himself while playing with the Edmonton Oilers.

In fact, he won five Stanley Cups in Edmonton, and only one on Seventh Avenue in Gotham.

But, New York being New York, the 1994 Stanley Cup championship was of such magnitude—check out the Canyon of Heroes parade—that it obliterated anything done in the North Country.

Messier's introduction to the ice game was immediate. Born in Edmonton on January 18, 1961, Mark soon learned that his father, Doug, was a minor league hockey defenseman of note.

153

For Mark and his brother, Paul, hockey was the only thing that they wanted to do. "Like any other kid, I wanted to be like my dad," Messier said, "and my brother and I took to [the game] naturally."

Even before he was eligible to join the NHL, Messier had a pro-like physique. By the time Mark was 17 years old, he stood 6'0" and weighed 195 pounds. Instead of waiting to join the NHL, Moose decided to play in the rival World Hockey Association during the 1978–79 season.

When the WHA folded at season's end, Mark was selected in the third round of the 1979 NHL Entry Draft by his hometown Oilers, who jumped from the WHA to the NHL for the 1979–80 season.

"You could see right away that he was going to be a good player," said former Oilers coach and general manager Glen Sather. "He had lots of fire in his heart."

In Edmonton, Messier was one of many young stars who formed the nucleus of an emerging dynasty. Messier played alongside players such as Paul Coffey, Jari Kurri, Glenn Anderson, Kevin Lowe, Grant Fuhr, and, of course, Wayne Gretzky.

With Gretzky and Messier forming a formidable 1-2 punch at center, the Oilers won four Stanley Cups in five seasons between 1984 and 1988. In the process, Messier emerged as the league's premier power forward, and was arguably as important to the Oilers' success as "The Great One."

"He was like Gordie Howe," said Jim Matheson, who has covered the Oilers for the *Edmonton Journal* since their days in the WHA. "Mess had the wicked elbows [like Gordie did]. He was the toughest good player in the league at that time."

Messier's chance to escape Gretzky's shadow came when No. 99 was traded to the Los Angeles Kings in the summer of 1988. Replacing Gretzky as Edmonton's captain, Messier led the Oilers to their fifth Stanley Cup in 1990, winning the Hart Trophy as the NHL's Most Valuable Player and recording a career-high 129 points during the regular season.

But after five Stanley Cups in seven seasons as an Oiler, Messier was ready for a new challenge. Mark would find that on Broadway, where the Rangers hadn't won a Stanley Cup since 1940.

"New York was the only place that I could envision myself coming to," Messier said. "The challenge of [trying to win a Cup in New York], playing for an Original Six team, and living in New York City seemed to be exactly what I wanted."

However, there were doubts about whether Messier—who was 30 years old in 1991—would be the same type of player. It was Sather who assured Rangers GM Neil Smith that Messier was as good as advertised.

"To me, Mark was the best player in the league at that time," Sather said. "I told Smith that this was the guy who was going to win the Stanley Cup for him."

The trade was completed on October 4, 1991, as the Rangers sent Bernie Nicholls, Louie DeBrusk, Steven Rice, and $15 million to Edmonton. When Messier arrived in Montreal the next day, both players and media alike were in awe of the five-time Cup champion.

"I remember he was skating around and I was on the other side of the ice," said Brian Leetch. "I said to James Patrick, 'Can you believe Mark Messier is on the ice with us? Can you believe he is on our team?'"

"Messier brought credibility to the franchise," WFAN's Chris "Mad Dog" Russo said. "He gave the Ranger fan hope that he was going to turn it around."

The Rangers instantly became Messier's team. That fact was cemented when he was named captain during the team's home opener. Mark's first year in New York was a success.

He led the Rangers to the league's top record in 1991–92, and won his second Hart Trophy as league MVP. However, the Rangers were ousted by the eventual champion Pittsburgh Penguins in the Patrick Division Finals.

The next season was one of Messier's toughest in New York. Despite having Stanley Cup expectations, the Blueshirts stumbled out of the gate, and a conflict between Messier and head coach Roger Neilson came to the surface.

Neilson was ultimately fired, but the Rangers' tailspin continued. The team would finish last in the Patrick Division, and the media and fans turned on the Blueshirts.

"Late in the season, Messier was actually booed," said Jeff Z. Klein, who covers the Rangers for *The New York Times* and authored the biography *Messier*. "It was probably the only time in his entire New York tenure that he was booed."

After missing the playoffs for the first time in his career, Messier was determined to get back to the postseason in 1993–94. With new head coach

Mike Keenan behind the bench, Messier led the Blueshirts to a franchise-record 52 wins and the Rangers won their second President's Trophy in three seasons.

It was in the playoffs where Messier would cement his legacy. The Rangers breezed through the first two rounds, but faced a formidable opponent in the New Jersey Devils in the Eastern Conference Finals.

The Rangers fell behind three games to two and faced elimination in Game 6 at the Meadowlands. In an attempt to galvanize his teammates, Messier put everything on the line and guaranteed that the Rangers would win.

"I thought, what a great idea it would be for all my teammates to read the paper as we always do, and open it up and see that I really believe that we can go to New Jersey and win," Messier said years later. "The slight overview on my part was when I realized that 14 million New Yorkers, the Devils, and the media were going to be reading the same thing."

"We all came into the room for the morning skate and, boom, it was in the paper," Devils goaltender Martin Brodeur said. "I thought, that's a little tough for him to go out and say that."

Through the first half of the game, the Devils made Messier eat his words. New Jersey had a 2–0 lead after the first period, and continued to dominate the Rangers in the second period. Keenan called a timeout midway through the period and didn't say a word.

Yet with the season unraveling, Messier brought the Rangers back from the precipice of defeat. First, he assisted on Alexei Kovalev's goal near the end of the period to cut the Devils' lead to 2–1.

Then Messier tied the game by beating Brodeur with a backhand shot early in the third. Later, with the teams skating four aside, Messier slammed home the rebound from a Kovalev shot to give the Rangers the lead.

To cap it off, with Brodeur at the bench and the Devils on a power play, Messier intercepted a pass in his own zone and fired a shot all the way down the ice into the empty net to complete the hat trick.

Messier's three goals and one assist led the Rangers to a 4–2 win and was one of the greatest individual performances in NHL history.

"When I was on the bench and I saw him shoot for the open net I said, 'Oh my god,'" Brodeur revealed. "It's the best story you could ever write, and he did it."

Mark Messier backed up his famous guarantee and finally brought the Cup back to New York in 1994. (AP Images)

"When Mark turned and shot the puck [down the ice], it hit me that he was going to get a hat trick," Rangers goalie Mike Richter said. "He was going to get the game-winner and a hat trick and he called the game. I could see history just sliding right down the ice."

Longtime New York broadcaster Spencer Ross said, "It was the closest thing I've ever seen in my life to one individual literally willing a team to victory. He made them win."

Coming off of "The Guarantee" win, the Rangers defeated the Devils in the second overtime of Game 7 to advance to the Stanley Cup Finals against the Vancouver Canucks.

The Rangers jumped out to a 3–1 series lead, but lost Games 5 and 6. In the decisive Game 7 at Madison Square Garden, Messier set up the game's first goal, and then scored the game-winner. The Messiah had delivered!

"It was a tremendous moment for me personally because I really came to New York with one objective and that was to help win a Stanley Cup," Messier said.

In the years that followed, Messier experienced great personal success, but the Rangers couldn't get back to the Finals. The closest the Blueshirts got was in 1996–97, when Messier and Gretzky led the Rangers on an improbable run to the Eastern Conference Finals, where they were derailed by the Flyers.

However, after the 1996–97 season, Messier and Garden management couldn't agree on a new contract, and "The Captain" packed his bags and signed with the Canucks.

Messier spent three years in Vancouver, but hardly enjoyed the same success he did in Edmonton and New York. When his contract expired after the 1999–2000 season, Mark came back to the Rangers, where he would spend the final four seasons of his career.

In 25 NHL seasons and 1,756 games, Messier tallied 694 goals, 1,193 assists, and 1,887 points, and won six Stanley Cups. He is the NHL's second-leading scorer—trailing only Gretzky—and is the only player to captain two different teams to a Stanley Cup championship.

But Messier's legacy in New York isn't defined by numbers.

"Messier is the man who killed 1940," Steve Politi of the *Newark Star-Ledger* said. "For Rangers fans, that's what they will remember the most."

Messier's No. 11 was retired by the Rangers on January 12, 2006, and he was inducted into the Hall of Fame in 2007.

chapter three

Wally Stanowski
The Oldest Living Ranger

BORN: Winnipeg, Manitoba, April 28, 1919

POSITION: Defenseman, Toronto Maple Leafs, 1939–42, 1944–48; New York Rangers, 1948–51

AWARDS/HONORS: NHL First Team All-Star, 1941; NHL All-Star Game, 1947

On April 28, 2013, Wally Stanowski celebrated his 94th birthday. He's the oldest living Ranger, topping his teammate from the 1949–50 squad, Edgar Laprade, by five months.

They remain significant in Rangers annals for various reasons. A onetime First All-Star defenseman, Stanowski solidified the Blueshirts backline and helped guide New York into what was then a rare playoff berth in 1950.

Laprade nearly won the Stanley Cup in the first overtime of Game 7 at Olympia Stadium in Detroit. "I had a breakaway," recalled the nifty center, "and beat Harry Lumley with my shot. But it hit the post and bounded out. Then the Wings scored in the second overtime and we were out."

Both Stanowski and Laprade agreed that their Rangers' days were the happiest of their hockey lives. Edgar spent his entire NHL career playing for the Big Apple's sextet. By contrast, Stanowski spent most of his years with the Maple Leafs, yet he insisted in an interview with me in April 2013 that he enjoyed being a Ranger much more than playing in Toronto.

"I liked the Rangers better than Toronto as a team. I liked the city [Manhattan], too. The man who brought me down to New York was Frank Boucher, who managed the Rangers at the time. I really liked Boucher. He was a very fine individual; in fact, there were none finer than Frank. He gave me some good years in New York.

"One of the things I liked about Manhattan was going into magic shops to buy trick cards; anything to entertain my teammates. Anything for a couple of laughs."

As for Stanowski's toughest foe, that was easy for him to answer.

"There's no doubt," Wally concluded, "that Maurice Richard was the most difficult person for me to defend against. He was a very powerful skater and very difficult to knock off his feet. His physical strength was immense. He was the hardest player to stop. Period.

"Also, when Max and Doug Bentley played alongside Bill Mosienko on Chicago's Pony Line, they gave me the heebie-jeebies."

This was a long way from Stanowski's Winnipeg childhood days during the Great Depression.

Eventually, he became a teenage star, helping the St. Boniface Seals score a pair of rare upsets in 1938, defeating the defending Memorial Cup champion Winnipeg Monarchs and then the heavily favored Oshawa Generals. Stanowski's brilliant end-to-end rushes as well as hard-hitting defensive work led to his eventual signing with the Toronto Maple Leafs in 1939.

"Wally," Hall of Fame author Frank Orr once said, "was the NHL's best rushing defenseman with the Maple Leafs. He had a superb free-wheeling skating style."

Although Stanowski played on four Stanley Cup winners with the Maple Leafs, he welcomed the trade to New York in 1948 because he believed that Leafs boss Conn Smythe had treated him shabbily despite Wally's skilled performances.

"The Toronto organization was cheap," Stanowski insisted, "while the Rangers weren't afraid to spend money. Plus, we had a terrific boss in Boucher, and in 1949–50 when we went to the final round against Detroit, our coach, Lynn Patrick, was top-notch."

New York fans enjoyed Stanowski's happy-go-lucky style but the laughter ended when a serious injury forced his NHL retirement in 1951, although he later resumed skating as a member of the NHL Old-Timers. Still spry, Wally skated alongside younger Hall of Famers such as Andy Bathgate, who also had played for both the Leafs and Rangers.

"It was tough getting Wally off the ice," Bathgate said after one Old-Timers game, "because he'd play double shifts if they let him. Once Wally said that if we couldn't rent the ice for practice, we should just rent the dressing room for the needling session—and a couple of beers!"

Stanowski admitted that one of his most pleasant, lasting memories took place when the old Madison Square Garden on Eighth Avenue between 49th and 50th streets finally closed in 1968.

Wally Stanowski, seen here standing on the right playing against the Chicago, is the oldest living Ranger. He was born on April 28, 1919.

Stanowski was thrilled when the Blueshirts organization invited him along with a number of stars from yesteryear to the final game at the old Garden.

"I was touched," Wally remembered, "because there were stars like Rocket Richard, Sid Abel, Gordie Howe, Syl Apps, and Ted Lindsay all there. We saw the last game on February 11, 1968, and they treated us all to dinner, and after the game, we met at a hotel bar across the street for more drinks and fun. It was an unforgettable night."

One report of the on-ice festivities included this sentence: "Wally Stanowski, renowned for his end-to-end rushes, also produced a roar from the crowd with his dipsy-doodle skating routine."

Stanowski was hailed then, and those who remember his entertaining stay with the Rangers hail him now as the oldest living Ranger!

Part V
The Present

| chapter one |

Henrik Lundqvist
The King of New York

BORN: Åre, Sweden, March 2, 1982

POSITION: Goalie, New York Rangers, 2005–Present

AWARDS/HONORS: Vezina Trophy, 2012; NHL First Team All-Rookie, 2006; NHL First Team All-Star, 2012; NHL All-Star Game, 2009, 2011–12

The unofficial anthem of New York City—alias, Gotham or the Big Apple—happens to be "New York, New York."

It also could be the theme song for Henrik Lundqvist.

As the lyrics in "New York, New York" indicate, if you can make it big on Broadway, you can make it big *anywhere* in the world.

The Rangers' Swedish-born goaltender not only won the 2012 Vezina Trophy as the National Hockey League's best goaltender, he was also knighted by the world's toughest media as "King Henrik," and that affectionate label has been in place for several illustrious seasons.

"The Rangers certainly felt Lundqvist was good enough to be an NHL player," longtime Rangers play-by-play man Sam Rosen says, "but I don't think anyone had the idea or could have predicted that he would come so far so fast."

However, Lundqvist's ascension to New York stardom was not an easy one. In fact, it's even more remarkable considering where the Swedish netminder had been before defending the home team's net in Madison Square Garden.

Henrik, along with twin brother, Joel, were born on March 2, 1982, in the small town of Åre, Sweden.

"It's a really small town up in northern Sweden," Lundqvist explains. "Everybody up there skis, and my dad was a ski instructor when I was growing up.

"When my brother and I were eight years old, we started to play hockey."

Lundqvist's start as a goaltender is owed to Joel, who would go on to play in the NHL with the Dallas Stars.

"Before the first game, the coach asked all of the guys if somebody wanted to be a goalie, and I just raised Henrik's arm and said, 'He wants to,'" Joel said.

"The first two games we played, we lost 12–2 and 18–0. He had a tough start, but he was pretty happy to be in goal anyway."

Henrik quickly rose through the Swedish ranks, becoming one of the best goalies in the nation. In 1999, the year before he was eligible for the NHL Draft, Lundqvist caught the eye of Blueshirts scout Jan Gajdosik.

"Before the tournament, I had never heard his name," Gajdosik admitted. "But he was just phenomenal in that tournament.

"I remember that in my report, I wrote, 'I've never seen a better European goalie at his age since Dominik Hasek.'"

Despite the high praise, Lundqvist wasn't picked immediately in the 2000 NHL Draft. In fact, Lundqvist wasn't taken until the seventh round, when the Rangers took him with the 205th pick overall.

"As you get deeper into the draft, you're basically looking for anyone with a heartbeat who can stand up and skate," said Don Maloney, who was the Rangers' assistant general manager in 2000.

"You're never thinking, *Let's wait until the seventh round to draft our franchise goaltender.* You're just throwing darts."

Although he was now Rangers property, Lundqvist didn't envision heading to North America. After he was drafted he continued to play for the Frolunda Indians, who played in Elitserien, Sweden's top pro hockey league.

Henrik's breakout year came in 2004–05, when the NHL was halted by a lockout that would wipe out the entire year.

"The lockout year was when the Rangers began to think that they may have been on to something with Lundqvist," former Rangers defenseman and analyst Dave Maloney said.

During that season, many NHL players (skaters and goalies alike) played in Elitserien. Lundqvist dominated the league, as he won league MVP and led the Indians to the championship.

At that point, Lundqvist was ready for a new challenge. "I didn't feel that I had to do more in Sweden," Henrik explained.

The Rangers signed Lundqvist in July of 2005, but nobody expected him to be the Blueshirts' top netminder with Kevin Weekes in the fold. Still, Lundqvist made an indelible impression on players, coaches, and the media alike in his first NHL training camp.

"He moved side to side as fast as any goalie I've ever seen, and this was within five minutes of seeing him live for the first time," said Andrew Gross, who covers the Rangers for the *Bergen Record*.

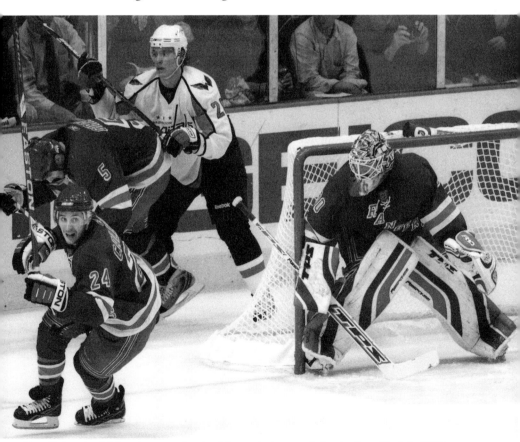

Henrik Lundqvist has been a standout in goal since arriving in New York in 2005.
(David Perlmutter)

Lundqvist started the season as the backup, but after Weekes suffered a groin injury in the fourth game of the season, Henrik started the next three games at Madison Square Garden—all Rangers wins.

Before the three-game stretch ended, Lundqvist was given his "King Henrik" moniker, and the fans were chanting his name inside MSG.

"That year was so much fun," Henrik recalled. "I really enjoyed playing in the Garden. The fans supported me from the start and that helped me a lot."

What also made that year fun was the Winter Olympics, which were held in Turin, Italy. As Sweden's starting goaltender, Lundqvist carried a nation's hopes on his back and led his country to a gold medal.

"Growing up, the Swedish national team was what we saw on television," Lundqvist said, "so it was a dream come true to play for Sweden. Having the gold medal is something that will always be there, and something that I will always remember."

After resuming the NHL season, Lundqvist set a Rangers rookie record by winning 30 games in 2005–06 and earning a Vezina Trophy nomination as one of the league's three top goaltenders. In addition, Henrik helped lead the Rangers to the postseason for the first time since the 1996–97 season.

The netminder built on his debut year by earning Vezina nominations in each of the next two seasons, while becoming the Rangers' MVP along the way as well.

"The first three years, it was a lot about proving to everybody else that I should be here, that I should play in this league," Lundqvist explained.

In addition to his stellar on-ice play, Lundqvist has captured New York off the ice. His interests in fashion and music have put him on places other than the back page of the Big Apple's newspapers.

However, his ascension to the Broadway stage has not taken his focus away from his work on the ice.

"The funny thing about Henrik is when you first get to meet him, you see a matinee idol and rock guitarist," *Newsday's* Steve Zipay said.

"When you get to know him a little bit, you realize he's got focus, concentration, and he battles every game.

"That combination is really what Rangers fans love."

Lundqvist has been the backbone of the Blueshirts' success since his arrival. He has been selected as the team's Most Valuable Player for six consecutive seasons, a Rangers record.

Lundqvist has also won at least 30 games in each of his first seven NHL seasons, which is an NHL record.

One of the keys to Lundqvist's success is his work ethic and competiveness, which extends beyond the games themselves.

"You could see the intensity in his eyes before we'd even go on the ice," said Steve Valiquette, who was Lundqvist's backup in New York from 2007 to 2009.

Henrik never likes to get beat—even in practice—and he has been known to trash a locker room on a night where his play wasn't up to par.

That competitive edge paid off for Lundqvist in spades in 2011–12, when King Henrik established career bests in wins (39), goals-against average (1.97), and save percentage (.930), and led the Rangers to their first Atlantic Division title since the club's Stanley Cup year in 1994.

In fact the goaltender from that 1994 Cup-winning team—and Lundqvist's predecessor—Mike Richter was impressed with the Swede's slick play in between the pipes.

"He's been nothing short of sensational," Richter said. "He's really enjoyable to watch and he's definitely one of the elite goalies in the league."

Lundqvist's elite status was recognized league-wide when he was awarded the Vezina Trophy in 2012. However, despite finishing the regular season with the most points in the Eastern Conference, the Rangers were ousted in six games by the New Jersey Devils in the conference finals.

"There were so many things that happened during the year that made it feel like that year could be something special," Lundqvist reflected after the season ended. "I hope it's a sign for something good that is coming."

Lundqvist followed up his award-winning campaign with a fitting encore during the lockout-shortened season in 2013. However, the year didn't start out that way for Hank, who needed a couple of games to find his rhythm.

"Every year, I never feel good during the preseason," Lundqvist revealed, "and that's usually three or four games. It's definitely not an excuse, but I needed to keep pushing myself to get to where I should be."

After the first three games of the regular season, Henrik's statistics were *better* than the year before. The Rangers needed Lundqvist to be as spectacular as he was, since the offense wasn't as prolific as anticipated at the start of the year.

Between March 18 and April 6, Lundqvist didn't allow more than two goals in any contest over a 10-game stretch and kept the Rangers in playoff contention.

Lundqvist won the Vezina Trophy as the NHL's top goaltender in 2012.
(David Perlmutter)

"I felt pressure to not make too many mistakes," Lundqvist said during the streak. "We needed the points and we weren't scoring a ton. I just needed to focus on every game and try to be even better to give us a better chance to win."

Despite the outstanding numbers, Lundqvist was still searching for an elusive shutout during the season. The whitewash eventually came during a monumental, heart-stopping 1–0 overtime victory over the rival Islanders at Nassau Coliseum on April 13. Not only did Henrik's 29 saves keep the Rangers in the game throughout, it enabled the Blueshirts to creep closer to the Isles in the standings.

"It was about time I shut the door completely," Lundqvist said after the shutout. "I was playing well but I needed some puck luck, too."

That puck luck came in the form of a few posts and crossbars, including one shot from Casey Cizikas, who hit the post with three minutes remaining in the second period.

Lundqvist also made a decisive save on Matt Moulson early in the first period. The three-time 30-goal scorer had a prime rebound chance in front of the net, but Lundqvist stopped the shot with his glove, and then swatted the puck to the corner with his stick.

"I kept reminding myself to be ready, and that the next goal was going to be the game-winner," Lundqvist recalls. "I couldn't afford to make a mistake."

The victory on Long Island propelled the Rangers to a 6–2 record down the stretch. They would reach the playoffs as the sixth seed in the Eastern Conference.

Lundqvist was selected as the club's Most Valuable Player for the seventh season in a row—a franchise record—as he finished the year with 24 wins (tied for most in the league), a 2.05 goals-against average, and a .926 save percentage.

What's more, Henny received the fifth Vezina Trophy nomination of his eight-season career.

"It was an interesting year [2012–13]," Lundqvist reflected after the season. "It was different because of the shorter season and tighter schedule. A lot of things went our way last year, but this year we had to work really hard for it.

"I always try to push myself as much as possible. I want to be up there and be recognized as a good goalie. When people recognize what you do, it's always a fun thing."

The Blueshirts' first-round opponent in the 2013 playoffs was the Southeast Division champion Washington Capitals, led by one of the most prolific scorers in the NHL, Alexander Ovechkin.

Lundqvist was no stranger to Washington in the playoffs. The Rangers defeated the Caps in seven games the year before, and 2013 marked the fourth time in five seasons that the two teams squared off in the postseason.

Despite Lundqvist's best efforts, the Rangers lost the first two games in Washington, and trailed 3–2 in the series heading into Game 6 at Madison Square Garden.

Facing elimination, Henrik delivered the best playoff performances of his career. On back-to-back nights, Lundqvist stopped all 62 shots he faced, leading the Rangers to a 1–0 victory in New York in Game 6 and a 5–0 triumph over the Caps in Washington in Game 7.

It was the first time in the Rangers' 87-year history that the team had won a Game 7 on the road.

"You make your legacy as a player in these types of situations," then-Rangers head coach John Tortorella said. "The ultimate goal for Hank is to win a Stanley Cup, but you need to go through these types of situations to get there. He's certainly come up big for us."

So far, so good!

chapter two

Ryan Callahan
The Captain

BORN: Rochester, New York, March 21, 1985

POSITION: Right Wing, New York Rangers, 2006–Present

The template for the ideal captain was set by the original Blueshirt, right wing Bill Cook, who starred for New York's first two Stanley Cup teams.

Art Coulter, the defenseman who helped guide the New Yorkers to their third Cup in 1940, was no less admirable as a leader of men.

Others who followed suit with consummate skill and courage were the likes of Don "Bones" Raleigh, who scored two sudden-death goals in the 1950 Finals against Detroit, not to mention the inimitable Mark Messier, the man mostly responsible for the 1994 Cup victory.

Finding someone with the qualities of the aforementioned would not be easy, and that explains why Ryan Callahan has been such an ideal choice to wear the captain's "C."

Chosen as a relative afterthought in the fourth round (127th overall) of the 2004 NHL Draft, "Captain Cally" became a homegrown Blueshirt through and through. Despite his late-round draft status and his diminutive size (5'11"), Callahan's indefatigable work ethic propelled him through the ranks of the Rangers' farm system and into the Broadway spotlight.

After four years in the OHL and several temporary callups from the AHL's Hartford Wolfpack, Ryan eventually proved himself irreplaceable to the big club. From the outset of his professional career, he has always finished tops in hits, often matching up against players with several dozen pounds on him. What's more, this feisty kid could put up the points as well.

A knee injury sidelined the 22-year-old Callahan at the beginning of the 2007–08 campaign, and he was sent down to Hartford on a conditioning stint to help him return to top form. On February 3, 2008, Cally was recalled from the AHL to replace an injured Brendan Shanahan. The gutsy Rochester, New York, winger took to the ice that night and never looked back.

Callahan's breakout season in 2008–09 began with a climactic series-clinching goal in the inaugural Victoria Cup tournament, which pitted the Rangers against the KHL's Metallurg Magnitogorsk during the NHL's pre-season. Exhibiting his classic combination of tenacity and skill, Cally went on to pot 22 goals that year, matching then-captain Chris Drury for third-best on the team.

Callahan recorded similar numbers the following season, but his true measure of indispensability to the team became evident in the 2010–11 campaign. Despite missing 19 games with a broken hand and three for a fractured ankle, he finished second on the team in scoring. Both injuries were a result of successfully blocked shots, cementing Callahan's image as a true on-ice warrior.

Soon enough, Ryan began to garner attention for his passionate, dogged style of play. On April 8, 2009, Callahan was presented with the Steven McDonald Extra Effort Award, given annually to the Blueshirt who is believed to perform "above and beyond the call of duty" night in and night out. He would go on to earn the award again in 2009–10, 2011–12, and 2012–13, joining Adam Graves as the only players to capture the prestigious honor four or more times.

"You can reach a certain level based on skill and talent," *Newsday* reporter Steve Zipay assessed of Callahan. "And then to really make a mark, there's that intangible. Callahan has it."

Callahan's gritty style of play endeared him to management and fans alike, as he hurled his body in front of incoming slap shots with reckless abandon. In his first five NHL seasons, Callahan consistently finished tops in the league in blocked shots and hits, despite his small frame.

When Callahan was named the 26th captain in New York Rangers history on September 12, 2011, the appointment came as a surprise to no one.

Captain Cally had become the team's heart and soul, the soft-spoken, loud-action leader on and off the ice. What's more, Ryan's blood was even Bluer than most as a homegrown captain twice over: he is both a Rangers original draft pick and a New York state native, the only Blueshirt captain to boast that résumé.

The stage was now set for the 2011–12 season. Would the young captain rise to the occasion or crumble under the pressure?

Fortunately for the Blueshirts, Callahan came out of the gate with flying colors.

The Rochester native immediately set the tone for what was to come under his stewardship, scoring the team's first goal of the season in his first game wearing the "C."

All-Star defenseman Dan Girardi praised Callahan's natural leadership ability. "He says a lot in the dressing room, but he leads more with his on-ice play—blocking shots, hitting guys, scoring goals," Girardi explained.

Callahan continued to dominate physically, once again jumping to the head of the NHL pack in hits and blocked shots. But he also continued to dominate offensively, finishing the season with a career-high 29 goals, 13 on the power play. He also demonstrated a propensity for scoring the right goals at the right time; in locker room lingo, for being unfailingly "clutch."

Then-coach John Tortorella noted that because of everything else he does on the ice, Ryan's skill tends to go unnoticed: "You talk about Ryan Callahan, you call him a grinder. And he is. But he gets overlooked as far as his offensive abilities and his talent, because the other stuff sticks out. But that's why he's our captain, and that's how he leads us."

The captain went on to score a whopping nine game-winning goals (and a couple of key shootout winners) in 2011–12, tying the franchise record along with Brad Richards. To add to the mounting excitement surrounding Callahan's career, several of his game-winners were scored in particularly dramatic fashion.

Solidifying himself as a true team player, Callahan's personal career milestones retained significance on the club level as well. To secure the franchise's 2,500th regular season victory on December 10, 2011, Ryan broke into the Buffalo Sabres' zone on a penalty kill and executed a nifty spin-o-rama, slipping the puck past goalie Jhonas Enroth for the game-winning goal.

Ryan Callahan was named the 26ᵗʰ captain in Rangers history in 2011.
(David Perlmutter)

In another matchup against Buffalo, Callahan netted his 100th career NHL goal in overtime to yet again seal the win for the Blueshirts. And to cap off a career season as his team made the push for the Eastern Conference title, Cally's second overtime winner of the season sent the Detroit Red Wings packing with a howitzer from the slot—his 27th goal on his 27th birthday!

More often than not, Callahan single-handedly dominated penalty kills, diving in front of enemy slap shots and stealing the puck from opponents with Selke-worthy defensive skill.

"Whenever he's not on the ice, he's missed, and you notice he's not there," teammate Brian Boyle raved to former NHL.com reporter Dave Lozo. "And when he's on the ice, you notice that he's making big plays."

When the second-year captain suffered a shoulder injury in the sixth game of the shortened 2013 season, his team practically imploded. The Rangers were blanked by the Penguins 3–0 in the first game without their do-it-all captain, and true to Boyle's words, Callahan was noticeable in his absence on the ice. He was needed when the Blueshirts went 0-for-4 on the power play, and he was missed on the team's top penalty-killing unit, which gave up a power-play goal to the Pens early in the third period.

For his part, Callahan didn't hold any ill will toward Max Talbot, the culprit behind his injured shoulder, instead chalking up his injury to bad luck. "Fighting is a part of the game, and if it presents itself again, then you have to do it," the captain told Zipay.

While his team continued to struggle during a 4–3 loss to the Winnipeg Jets on February 26, Cally was one of the few bright spots. On a particularly memorable shift, the captain blocked two shots and threw two hits all without a stick, and the deafening roar of the Garden faithful expressed appreciation for his awe-inspiring actions.

"He tried to will us to a win," Tortorella marveled. "He was this close to getting us a point. Ryan Callahan is that type of player, we all know that. He is a special guy."

Many skaters stepped up their game over the course of the 2012–13 season, but when the team needed a goal most, it turned to its captain.

After a tumultuous campaign in which the Rangers never truly seemed to find consistency, the team's playoff hopes were hanging by a gossamer string in the final few games of the season. In the third-to-last game, the Blueshirts dropped a 3–2 decision to the cellar-dwelling Florida Panthers, making the next game against the Carolina Hurricanes even more significant.

The Rangers were all business starting the game. They potted two goals in the first period and controlled most of the action. But Carolina would not back down, and the teams headed into the third period tied 2–2.

Just 49 seconds into the third period, Jiri Tlusty struck again for the Canes, putting the home club up 3–2. Rangers fans were suitably concerned. The minutes were ticking away, and so were their playoff hopes.

In hockey, luck works in mysterious ways. And with less than three minutes remaining in the contest, luck finally seemed to be on the Rangers' side. Carolina was handed a penalty, and on the power play, Brad Richards sent a shot caroming off the boards. Incredibly, the puck bounced off the wall and hit goaltender Dan Ellis' skate, redirecting right into the net.

The Broadway Blueshirts were alive and the game remained knotted at 3–3 at the final horn, prompting overtime. The Rangers had gained a point, but needed another to clinch a playoff spot. Enter Captain Callahan, stage right.

After Henrik Lundqvist made several key saves to start the extra session, the puck remained in the Rangers' zone. Finally, Derek Stepan chipped the rubber out to a streaking Callahan, who floated along the left boards with nary an angle at which to shoot.

From the bottom of the faceoff circle, he fired a wrister toward the right post—and in! His teammates mobbed him enthusiastically, celebrating the franchise's seventh playoff berth in eight years. And it was due in large part to the ultimate captain.

"It couldn't be more fitting that he was the one to score the winner," Tortorella grinned.

Like fine wine, Ryan Callahan continues to improve with age, and New York fans have had the pleasure of watching him mature as a player and a leader before their eyes. A prototypical sparkplug, Captain Cally embodies the new Rangers' identity, carrying with him the hopes of an energetic Blueshirts team.

Ryan's older brother, Mike, noted that Callahan's personality combined with his style of play are what make him successful both on and off the ice. "He might not be the biggest kid or the best player," said the proud big brother, "but when he puts his heart and mind to it, he can accomplish anything."

| chapter three |

Dan Girardi
The Defender

BORN: Welland, Ontario, April 29, 1984

POSITION: Defenseman, New York Rangers, 2006–Present

AWARDS/HONORS: NHL All-Star Game, 2012

When all-purpose Rangers defensemen from yesteryear are discussed, the names of Ivan "Ching" Johnson, Murray "Muzz" Patrick, Art "Trapper" Coulter, and Lou "The Leaper" Fontinato come to mind.

Among the contemporary Blueshirts blueliners, the individual who comes closest to being a reasonable facsimile of yesterday's heroes is Welland, Ontario, native Dan Girardi.

What's inspiring about his nowhere-to-somewhere saga is that he was a total unknown, overlooked by all 30 National Hockey League teams when Girardi was available to be drafted between the ages of 18 and 20.

His ascent to the NHL involved a circuitous route from such diverse towns as Guelph, London, Barrie, Charlotte, and Hartford.

Even when he reached Manhattan's Seventh Avenue, the experts' prevailing opinion was that he was only up for the proverbial cup of coffee.

The good news is that he is still sipping the java as a core defenseman for the Rangers and the apple of the Big Apple's hockey eye.

Kudos go out to the Rangers' scouts who signed the undrafted gem to a professional contract in the summer of 2006, but Dan Girardi's steady rise to stardom was just as much a result of his own hard work and resilience. "Growing up in Welland, it's really a small, close-knit community," explained Girardi, who worked as a dishwasher in a Chinese restaurant growing up, "and that's where I learned what hard work is."

Dan also credited his parents, Mark, an assembly line worker at General Motors, and Carol, a nurse, for instilling him with an unflappable work ethic. Since breaking out on Broadway, Dan's blue-collar identity has endeared him to Rangers fans and cemented his position at the core of the Blueshirts' back line.

"My dad and I would just shoot buckets of pucks, all day," he reminisced. "I'm still working on things that he showed me."

After going undrafted and spending 231 career games in the OHL and 118 career games with the Hartford Wolfpack (AHL) and Charlotte Checkers (ECHL), it seemed as if Girardi was destined to be a career minor leaguer. But someone in the Rangers organization took notice of the promising young defenseman. In April of 2006 Girardi earned the Wolfpack's "Unsung Hero" award, and a few months later, he signed a contract with the Rangers as a free agent.

Captain Ryan Callahan, Girardi's teammate in Junior and current roommate on the road, reflected on his buddy's rise to stardom: "To be honest, I didn't know he was going to grow up to be this type of player and be this good. We always knew he was good at that level, but the strides he's taken in the last couple of years have been pretty amazing."

Even after signing his first professional contract, Dan's jump to the big league wasn't a given. He was sent down immediately following his first training camp with the Blueshirts. But as his mother, Carol, noted, "The rejections made him even more motivated."

On January 27, 2007, Girardi was called up from the Hartford Wolf Pack to the Rangers because of an injury to Darius Kasparaitis. Jim Schoenfeld, the Wolf Pack's general manager and one of Girardi's earliest and most vocal supporters, called Dan into his office and told him, "I hope I never see you again."

Six NHL seasons and 488 NHL games later, Girardi would never again don a Hartford Wolf Pack jersey. What's more, over his first five full seasons, he only missed two games, sitting out with a rib injury.

Girardi's ironman streak is even more impressive given the nature of his game. Girardi routinely ranks among the top shot-blockers and hitters of the league. In 2010–11, Dan led the entire NHL with 236 blocked shots—a whopping 24 more than the player just behind him in the rankings.

His willingness to sacrifice his body for the sake of the game defies all logic, but speaks to the kind of indomitable player that he is.

Rangers amateur scout Rich Brown related a story about Girardi from the 2005 OHL playoffs. The blueliner had casually mentioned some soreness in his right hand after blocking a shot on a shift, but he merely taped up his hand and carried his Knights through the next three playoff rounds. When Girardi finally had his hand X-rayed after the Knights' first Memorial Cup win, the picture was clear: his hand was broken.

"That shines a light on the type of character he has," Brown told Katie Strang of ESPNNewYork.com, "and his will to win."

The other mark of Girardi's game has been, and continues to be, his unwavering dependability. "He's Mr. Consistency," teammate Marc Staal noted to Sean Hartnett of CBS. "He's either good or great every night." Added Callahan: "You can always rely on him in all situations. When he's back there, he logs a lot minutes for us and is out there in key situations."

In February of 2011, Staal, the Rangers alternate captain and esteemed top defenseman, suffered a concussion after a hit by his brother, Eric, of the Carolina Hurricanes. Though Marc played the remainder of the season, it was revealed before the start of the 2011–12 campaign that he would not be available to start the season with the squad. This gaping hole on New York's top line of defense provided the perfect opportunity for Girardi to step up and demonstrate his value as being on par with his All-Star defense partner.

Coach John Tortorella was immediately impressed by the calm, steel-hearted blueliner and awarded Girardi with an alternate captaincy in Staal's absence. "He is a core foundation guy for us, and I'll put him with anybody as far as one of the top defensemen in our league," Tortorella raved.

Girardi proved that he was worth the letter on his jersey and then some. That season, Dan led all NHL skaters in average time on ice, logging close to a staggering 28 minutes a game. He earned the Rangers' nomination for the Bill Masterton Memorial Trophy, awarded annually to the player who "best exemplifies the qualities of perseverance, sportsmanship, and dedication to hockey."

Though he is less touted for his offensive prowess, "Danny G" has a scoring touch that tends to reveal itself in the clutch.

Dan Girardi has been a stalwart presence on New York's blueline; the defenseman has only missed two games in his first five seasons. (David Perlmutter)

As the truncated 2012–13 season was coming to a close, the Rangers finally seemed to break free of season-long inconsistencies and were focused on securing one of the Eastern Conference's final playoff spots. The rival Islanders were enjoying a similar push for the postseason, the team's first since 2007.

With the two area clubs suddenly neck and neck in the standings, the homestretch game on Saturday, April 13, would go a long way in deciding where both teams would finish at the end of the season.

"I tried to prepare for it like a playoff game, because it was that important," goalie Henrik Lundqvist confided to Pat Leonard of the *Daily News*.

That night, Nassau Veterans Memorial Coliseum was rocking in a playoff atmosphere. Many Blueshirts fans migrated from Manhattan to Uniondale to support the visiting team, and the game itself proved to be an epic heart-stopper despite—or perhaps because of—the scoreless tie at the end of regulation time.

At 3:11 of overtime, the tie was broken by a player whose versatile game had become a Rangers staple: Dan Girardi. The play unfolded when forward Derick Brassard carried the puck into the enemy zone and executed a nifty saucer pass to send Girardi in alone to confront Evgeni Nabokov.

"I just closed my eyes, shot it, and hoped for the best," Girardi quipped. "Seriously, I had two choices—I could either go short-side or fire it high to the left corner. I saw a lot of room up top, and that's where I wanted to put it; that's where it went."

The stalwart blueliner's wish was granted when his laser hit the bull's-eye behind Nabokov. It was Girardi's first career overtime goal and it secured the much-needed extra point for the Rangers.

Dan's first playoff goal came at a crucial time as well and proved to be the series winner in Game 7 of a heated 2012 first-round matchup with the Ottawa Senators. Unfailingly humble, Girardi naturally deflected praise and focused the spotlight on his team. "Anyone could have scored a goal in this game and been the hero," he said to Pat Leonard. "A lot of guys did a lot of little things that might have gone unnoticed."

If anyone knows anything about going unnoticed for doing a lot of little things, it's Girardi. But in January of 2012, one of the most underrated players in the National Hockey League finally got his moment of fame.

Girardi—alongside players such as Evgeni Malkin, Zdeno Chara, Shea Weber, and Pavel Datsyuk—was chosen to participate in the 2012 NHL All-Star Game. His selection was somewhat surprising given his lack of on-ice flair or bulging scoring stats, but the league-wide attention was a long time in coming.

"I think sometimes our league forgets about people like that," Tortorella pointed out. "That restores a little faith in me, that the league stepped up and gave credit where credit was due. It's not just pedigree. It's what he's done on the ice."

For this reason, Yahoo! Sports' Nick Cotsonika labeled Girardi "the anti–All-Star."

Five years previously, Girardi's only association with the NHL All-Star Game was getting the opportunity to practice with the big club during the All-Star break after his callup from Hartford. "It was pretty cool to be able to skate with guys like Jaromir Jagr and Brendan Shanahan," Dan reminisced.

Not only did he skate with them, but he proved he was able to compete with them as well. And when Girardi's name was listed along with Datsyuk, Malkin, and soon-to-be teammate Rick Nash, it was not because he could put up points like them or unleash a booming slap shot with killer accuracy, but because Dan Girardi was the one who's always there to shut them down.

chapter four

Rick Nash
The Missing Piece

BORN: Brampton, Ontario, June 16, 1984

POSITION: Left Wing, Columbus Blue Jackets, 2002–12; New York Rangers, 2012–Present

AWARDS/HONORS: Maurice Richard Trophy, 2004; NHL First Team All-Rookie, 2003; NHL All-Star Game, 2004, 2007–09, 2011

There's a comedy club in Times Square where one of the comedians has a bit that had perfect application to Rick Nash's trade to the Rangers in 2012.

As the comic tells it, two guys meet on the street and one of them has a large wooden mallet in his hands. Every few seconds the mallet-holder hits himself in the head with the oversized hammer.

The onlooker finally asks, "Why do you keep hitting yourself in the head with that large wooden mallet?"

To which the other replies with complete logic, "Because it feels so good when I stop!"

After playing for the underwhelming Columbus Blue Jackets for nine years, Nash could have been forgiven if he had developed chronic migraines. Over that span of time—he was named captain in 2008—the native of Brampton, Ontario, got a firsthand look at NHL ineptitude. The forlorn Ohio sextet made the playoffs only once—out in four straight games!—with no hope in sight.

Rick's salvation came when New York general manager Glen Sather dispatched forwards Brandon Dubinsky and Artem Anisimov, defenseman Tim

Erixon, and the Blueshirts' first-round pick in the 2013 NHL Draft to bring the 6'4" Nash to Seventh Avenue.

But what makes the hulking winger worth the asking price that the Rangers had to pay the Blue Jackets?

Well, the story of Nash's emergence to National Hockey League stardom begins during his Junior hockey days. Nash was selected fourth overall in the 2000 Ontario Hockey League Draft by the London Knights.

It was in London where Rick would don No. 61 for the first time in his career.

"I went to training camp and asked for number 13," Nash recalled. "They didn't allow it because of superstition. I then asked for 16 but a veteran already had it. At that point, I said it didn't matter to me, and whatever you put in my stall is fine.

"The next day I came in and 61 was in [the stall]."

With the new number on his back, Nash tore through the OHL. In two seasons with the Knights, the teenager tallied 63 goals and 138 points in just 112 games.

In the summer of 2002, the Blue Jackets selected Nash with the first overall pick in the NHL Entry Draft. Almost immediately, the forward became the face of the new Columbus franchise.

Nash quickly flourished in Columbus. During his second season, he became the youngest player to lead the NHL in goals, when he tied for the league lead with 41 tallies. That season—the 2003–04 campaign—Rick was also selected to the first of five All-Star Games he would play as a Blue Jacket.

Following the 2004–05 lockout, the power forward established himself as a perennial 30-goal scorer. Nash's combination of size and speed made it difficult for other teams to defend him.

In fact, the Ontario native incorporates the traits of his favorite Leafs players as a youth into his own game.

"I always looked up to guys like Wendel Clark, Doug Gilmour, and even Mats Sundin in later years," Nash said. "It was always fun to watch those guys."

Like his idols, Nash would become a captain of his franchise when he was given the "C" on March 12, 2008. Although he had personal success in his first five seasons, the Blue Jackets never reached the postseason. In Nash's first

Rick Nash arrived in New York with high expectations following a trade with the Columbus Blue Jackets in 2012. (David Perlmutter)

full season as captain, both he and the club reached the apex of Rick's tenure in Columbus.

Nash scored 40 goals and posted a career-high 79 points during the 2008–09 season, leading the Blue Jackets to their first playoff appearance in franchise history. Although the eventual Western Conference champion Detroit Red Wings would sweep Columbus in the first round, the experience was one that Nash savors to this day.

"When we clinched a playoff spot and brought the very first playoff game to Columbus, Ohio, it was exciting," Nash said. "Being with the franchise for six years, it was nice to finally achieve that."

However, the Blue Jackets were unable to build off of their playoff appearance. Columbus missed the playoffs in each of the next two seasons, and by the midway point of the 2011–12 season, Nash's name was circulating in trade rumors throughout the league.

Ultimately, Columbus agreed to trade their franchise player to the Blueshirts on July 23, 2012. Nash was enthusiastic about playing in Gotham.

"The Rangers are already one of the best teams in the league," Nash said at his introductory press conference. "For me to come on and help in any way I can made me want to play here.

"I'm embracing it all. This is what I feel is hockey. This is part of it. It makes the game that much more special."

Nash certainly didn't disappoint during his first season with the Rangers. His speed and size dazzled the Garden crowd, and the hulking forward put up impressive numbers throughout the year. His best stretch of the season was a 10-game point streak between February and March.

One game in particular that stood out was a late February contest at MSG against the Tampa Bay Lightning. After being sidelined for four games due to an undisclosed injury, Nash recorded a goal, an assist, and 12 shots on goal in a 4–1 Rangers victory. Even after the impressive performance, Nash was coy when it came to describing his outstanding night.

"I felt okay," Nash said after the game. "My timing was a bit off, but we got the two points, and that's all that matters."

It's that demeanor that led John Tortorella to call him a "low-maintenance" player.

"I think he's at a point in his career where this is the next step in his game," Tortorella said. "He comes to a bigger market, more pressure on him, trying to find his way to produce in the playoffs.

"He handled himself very well at Columbus. This is a different stage for him. I think this is perfect timing for Nash and the Rangers organization to have him here."

Tortorella has since moved on to become the head coach in Vancouver, but the best in Nash may come under new Rangers coach Alain Vigneault.

chapter five

Derek Stepan
The Future

BORN: Hastings, Minnesota, June 18, 1990

POSITION: Center, New York Rangers, 2010–Present

North of the border, the traditional journey to the ice game's highest level begins on the frozen ponds of rural areas. In the United States, most of the youth hockey players that reach the National Hockey League arrive via the "State of Hockey," also known as Minnesota.

That was the case for Rangers center Derek Stepan, whose climb up the ranks took him from Minnesota to Manhattan.

Stepan was born on June 18, 1990, in Hastings, Minnesota. Derek's father, Brad, was a fifth-round draft pick of the Blueshirts in 1985. Although the senior Stepan never played a game for the Rangers, he and Derek represent a rare father-son duo to be selected by the Blueshirts.

"He was a rink rat growing up," Brad says about Derek. "I never had to push him into hockey."

Stepan spent most his childhood playing on the outdoor rinks in Minnesota. "The biggest thing about playing outdoors is that the ice is more difficult to work with," Derek explains. "Pucks are harder, so if you get in the way it's going to hurt.

"When it comes to time to play in The Garden, I remember times playing outside because it is where I started."

Center Derek Stepan was drafted by New York in 2008 and became the first Ranger in team history to score a hat trick in his NHL debut in 2010. (David Perlmutter)

One of Derek's biggest decisions came when he was 16 years old and left his hometown to play high school hockey at renowned Shattuck St. Mary's. The school developed a number of NHL players, including the likes of Sidney Crosby and Jonathan Toews.

In Stepan's senior season, he registered 44 goals and 67 assists in just 60 games, and Shattuck won its second straight national championship. Derek's campaign impressed the Rangers enough to select him in the second round (51st overall) in the 2008 NHL Draft.

After being drafted, Stepan played two seasons at the University of Wisconsin, where he became a teammate of Ryan McDonagh. In two seasons with the Badgers, Stepan tallied 87 points in 81 games. In his sophomore season, Derek played in the national championship game, where the Badgers ultimately lost to Boston College.

But Derek's real burst into the spotlight came during the 2010 World Junior Championships in Canada. Serving as the captain of the U.S. squad, 19-year-old Stepan led all players in the tournament with 14 points (four goals, 10 assists) in seven games, and carried the Americans to a gold medal triumph over Team Canada.

"He was a major reason why we were so successful at World Juniors," said current Ranger Chris Kreider, who was also a teammate of Stepan during that tournament. "We weren't favored and he did an amazing job leading us. He gets people to come together…such a leader on and off the ice."

Coming off of such a successful season, the 20-year-old felt it was time to leave Wisconsin and head to New York. "For me it was the right move because I felt that I was ready for the next step," said Stepan.

"I have all the respect in the world for the University of Wisconsin, and it got me to where I am, but it just felt like the right move for me."

At Rangers camp in the fall of 2010, Stepan impressed coach John Tortorella enough to make the opening-night roster. His debut was one for the record books.

On October 9, 2010, against the Buffalo Sabres, Stepan scored a hat trick, becoming just the fourth player in NHL history to accomplish the feat in his first game. "Not a chance could I have dreamed this," said Stepan after the game. "You dream about playing in the NHL, and then you go out and play like that, I mean, the hockey gods must have been looking down on me.

"It was a fun night overall, that's for sure."

That fun night was the start of a solid freshman season for Stepan. The 20-year-old tallied 21 goals and 24 assists for 45 points, and finished fourth on the Rangers in goals and points. Additionally, he was fifth among rookies in the NHL in goals and points.

Derek followed up his rookie year with a better campaign in Year Two. Even with the acquisition of high-profile center Brad Richards, it was Stepan who centered the Blueshirts' most effective line throughout the 2011–12 season.

Playing alongside wingers Artem Anisimov and Marian Gaborik, the "G-A-S" line guided the Rangers to a first-place finish in the Eastern Conference. Stepan's playmaking abilities helped Gaborik have a bounce-back year, as the Slovakian lit the lamp 41 times.

Stepan finished the season with 17 goals and 34 assists, but—along with the rest of his teammates—struggled to score in the postseason. Derek only tallied one goal and eight assists in 20 playoff games, and the Blueshirts were eliminated by the cross-river rival Devils in the Eastern Conference Finals.

Tortorella was happy with Stepan's improvement, stating that he had a "good second year," but still saw more potential for the future.

"He was less inconsistent," Tortorella said when comparing Stepan's game from Year One to Year Two, "but I want to see more from him in the playoffs. He's a young kid and still learning, but I'd like him to be more consistent."

Derek answered the call in the shortened 2012–13 season. On a Rangers squad that struggled to score, Stepan was one of the bright spots. Once again, he centered the Blueshirts' most consistent line—playing alongside Carl Hagelin and newcomer Rick Nash—and averaged slightly less than a point per game.

"Each year I want to get better," Stepan said during the season. "I worked hard in the off-season to try to get myself in a situation where I can be better."

His coach recognized it, too, and at one point of the season, Tortorella referred to Stepan as one of the Rangers' top players.

"He's a guy that I use for all our guys that are struggling to find their games," Tortorella revealed about the young center. "[His success] was a great lesson for veteran guys, rookies…about how he goes about his business."

For Stepan, the improvement he showed in his third year was just a small step for the rest of his career. "I want to be a part of this organization for a long time," Derek enthused. "I want to win a Stanley Cup in New York."

The future is bright for the Minnesota kid who has acclimated himself to being an NHL player in Manhattan.

Part VI
The Making of a Fan

chapter one

How I Became a Rangers Fan
Two Oral Histories

Rangers fans come from all strata of society. Those who live in the New York metropolitan area represent a cross-section of rooters, from world-famous jazz critic Ira Gitler, who remembers the 1940 Stanley Cup–winning team, to housewife and mother Angela Sarro, whose late husband, Tom, was a teacher, historian, and a longtime season ticket holder.

In case you're wondering how a New Yorker becomes one of the Blueshirts faithful, the answers follow. A young female fan, Allyson Gronowitz, and her male counterpart, Michael Rappaport, provide a good example of how Rangers fans get that way.

Allyson Gronowitz: Raised in Section 424

I was both blessed and cursed to have been born to a longtime Rangers season ticket holder. My father, Steven, a gastroenterologist based in Clifton, New Jersey, had me waddling around with a hockey stick in my hand and a personalized Rangers jersey on my back before my second birthday. I grew up playing street hockey with my younger siblings, firing the bright orange ball into broken crates in our driveway all year long.

When I began high school, I immediately joined the girls floor hockey team, loving every minute of the game itself and the new friendships that came along with it. One such friend, Sara Klein, is largely responsible for introducing me to the excitement and promise of the Blueshirts of the early 2000s.

Sara, who remains one of my closest friends, invited me to go along with her to Rangers fan events and kept me up to date with the team's on-ice accomplishments. Under her tutelage, I began watching games—sometimes with her, sometimes at home with my father and brother. In school the next day, instead of discussing our favorite TV shows or gossiping about schoolmates, Sara and I would share our thoughts on the successes or failures of the New York Rangers and analyze what went right or wrong.

Sara also called my attention to one of the most creative, exciting, beloved Blueshirts during his stint on Broadway, and the player who would become largely singlehandedly responsible for cementing my lifelong devotion to the New York Rangers: a small Czech winger by the name of Petr Prucha.

I was immediately drawn to Prucha because of his diminutive size; as a small player myself, he was the perfect player for me to look "up" to. He soon won me over completely with his on-ice mixture of feisty energy and incomparable heart, and he opened my eyes to the delight of Broadway hockey.

Another player whose passion for the game inspired me was Brandon Dubinsky. I considered us both "Ranger Rookies," because Dubinsky's first year with the big club coincided with my first year as a full-time fan. To this date, the only Rangers jersey I have ever owned is a Dubinsky jersey, a coveted gift from my grandfather.

With my interest in the Blueshirts properly kindled, it only took one more push to send me over the edge for good. That push came in the form of my first playoff game, a match between the Rangers and the Buffalo Sabres on April 29, 2007, at the place that was soon to become my second home: Madison Square Garden.

The match was, as all playoff games are, a nailbiter. The indomitable Jaromir Jagr put the home team ahead 33 seconds into the second period, but Buffalo tied the game with less than eight minutes remaining to send both teams to overtime. I was experiencing my first playoff game, and I was about to experience my first 20-minute overtime. Then my first double overtime.

When Rangers defenseman Michal Rozsival found the net with a ferocious slap shot in the waning minutes of double overtime, I experienced

Allyson Gronowitz, devoted Rangers fan, splits her time between Teaneck, New Jersey, and Section 210 (formerly 424) at Madison Square Garden. (David Perlmutter)

a moment I will never forget: the "ping" of the puck on the inside crossbar signified the moment of silence before all bedlam broke loose. At the time, it propelled 18,200 electrified Blueshirts fans to their—*our*—feet, and the pure, exhilarating thrill of that instant after Rozsival scored was my "Eureka" moment: I knew, right then, that I was hooked for life.

After that, I began to attend as many games as I possibly could. Though I learned fairly quickly that the Rangers-Islanders rivalry was the stuff of legends, the Isles' luster had faded and there was a new bully in town: the appropriately named Devils. Since my birth in the early 1990s, the Devils had established their reputation as a perennial thorn in the side of the Broadway Blueshirts. For a girl growing up in Jersey, coming into school the day after a loss at the hands of the local Devils was crushing. When the Boys in Blue overcame the pesky Devils, though—was that ever gratifying. The 2008 Eastern Conference quarterfinals matchup was a particular favorite of mine, with the Rangers emerging with a decided four-games–to-one victory.

The Rangers got off to a remarkable start the following season, and one game early on stood out as particularly thrilling. Up until the last 10 seconds of the game, it appeared that New York was going to drop a 2–1 decision to the skilled and dominant Penguins. But Nikolai Zherdev had one more trick up his sleeve. As my father headed to the exit to beat the crowd, I—ever the purist—refused to leave until the buzzer sounded. The PA announcer informed the crowd that there was "One minute remaining in the game," and even as I stayed resolutely in my seat, I began to lose hope.

But with Henrik Lundqvist watching from the bench, Zherdev took a pass from Markus Naslund and sped past the blue line, rifling a shot over the glove of Marc-Andre Fleury with 8.3 seconds to go. I was shocked and euphoric, and I have always teased my father for nearly missing that goal! But the magical night wasn't over yet, as the Rangers took Pittsburgh to a shootout and Swedish speedster Fredrik Sjostrom netted the winner for the home team. My father and I left MSG that night later than expected, but infinitely happier as a result.

When I moved to Manhattan and Columbia University, I commandeered my father's season ticket package, arguing—correctly—that I would be frequenting the World's Most Famous Arena more often than anyone else in the family, since I now lived a mere subway ride away. There was one game, however, that I was forced to miss—my professor at Barnard College had the *chutzpah* to schedule a trip to the Metropolitan Opera the same night as a highly anticipated Bruins-Rangers game at MSG. As a result, I found myself twitching through an enigmatic storyline while squinting at an English translation on the screen in front of me, trying not to think about the exciting Original Six matchup taking place two dozen blocks downtown.

Around the time the second period began, I had come up with a plan. If I pulled up the Rangers website on my phone and put on my headphones, I'd be able to listen to the radio broadcast of the game. I hunched down in my seat and pulled on my hood so as to hide what I was doing from my peers, straining to hear the choppy feed of the game over the drama unfolding on stage at the Met.

My Blueshirts were down 3–0 with critical late-season playoff points on the line. I began to wonder where the bigger tragedy was taking place—at the Met or at Madison Square Garden. Czech winger Vinny Prospal potted two quick goals to put the Rangers within one, but three-quarters of the way into the third period New York was still a goal behind.

I sank lower in my seat. My eyes were following the action on the stage, but I had ears only for radio announcers Dave Maloney and Kenny Albert. With the clock ticking down, Ryan Callahan sent a pass along the boards to Brandon Dubinsky, who shocked everyone by swiftly putting the puck on his forehand and lofting it past Bruins goaltender Tim Thomas.

Though I only watched the highlights after the fact, I vividly remember trying to restrain myself from jumping up and down in the pitch-black silence around me. Luckily, Dave Maloney's shriek of excitement before announcing Dubinsky's game-tying goal expressed my feelings at that moment to a T. By the time Derek Stepan sealed the win with an empty-net goal (after Michael Sauer scored the go-ahead goal less than a minute after Dubinsky's tally), I had completely tuned out the opera, instead imagining myself a part of the celebratory scene at the Garden.

Another last-minute hair-raiser like the Rangers-Penguins game occurred in the 2012 playoffs when the stakes were much, much higher. The Blueshirts had a recent history of being run out of the postseason competition by the Washington Capitals, and with the Caps on the verge of taking a 3–2 series lead, this playoff race seemed no different. As my brother Mitchell and I watched dejectedly from my father's Blue Seats, the scoreboard displayed the 2–1 score in favor of the visitors, and the game was about to come to a close.

When Washington forward Joel Ward took a high-sticking penalty with a scant 22 seconds left, my brother and I barely dared to hope. The Rangers' power play was notoriously *un*powerful—what were the odds they'd manage to pull off the impossible in less than 30 seconds?

With the puck trapped in the offensive zone, the Rangers found themselves in a scramble in front of goalie Braden Holtby's net. Callahan took a swipe at the puck, but Holtby refused to yield. The captain collected his own rebound and tried again—still, no luck. Even a third shot on goal wasn't able to find the back of the net. The seconds were ticking by, as were New York's postseason aspirations.

Yet the black-and-Blueshirts were not about to give up. Brad Richards collected the loose puck for one last attempt—and, miraculously, the puck trickled off the right post and in.

It was pandemonium. The clock read 7.6 seconds and the score was now tied 2–2. I didn't realize I was holding my breath until I flew out of my seat to celebrate with the rest of the Garden faithful, yelling with both astonishment and joy. The triumphant pileup on the ice mirrored the scene in our section, as my brother nearly tumbled into the seats below us and, after regaining his footing, promptly began hugging and high-fiving every fan within sight. I was so exhilarated that I stood up for the entire intermission before overtime, and I was still standing 1:35 later, when Marc Staal scored on a slap shot from the point and sealed the victory for the home team.

Though the Rangers failed to bring home Lord Stanley's trophy that year, I will assuredly be right there when they do. From the Roszival slap shot to the Richards stuff-in, there have been many defining moments that solidified my devotion to the boys in blue. You know how it is: once you go Blue, you can never go back!

Michael Rappaport: Raised in Section 407

I have been a Rangers fan since birth. My dad likes to tell the story of how he held me in the hospital when I was one day old and the two of us watched the Blueshirts play on television.

Little did he or I know that this would be something we would continue to do through the first two decades of my life.

My first recollection of watching the Rangers was during the 1996–97 season, when I was five years old. It was the one season that Mark Messier and Wayne Gretzky shared the Broadway stage, and the Rangers made an improbable run to the Eastern Conference Finals.

Messier was my idol. My parents bought me numerous hockey VHS tapes once I got into the sport, and every single one featured a story on Messier and the Rangers' run to the Stanley Cup in 1994.

This made it even more disappointing when he left the Rangers as a free agent in the summer of 1997 and signed with the Vancouver Canucks.

My first game at MSG was when Messier returned to play the Rangers for the first time as a Canuck. I remember being in awe of the size of the building and the banners that filled the Garden rafters.

The night was an emotional one. The Rangers gave Messier a video tribute before the game—which he cried through—and he then scored a goal in the Canucks' 4–2 win.

There weren't too many high points through the next eight seasons. Starting with the year after Messier left, the Rangers missed the playoffs for seven consecutive seasons. During that time, the cross-river rival Devils won two Stanley Cups, and the Islanders made the playoffs three years in a row in the early 2000s. Going to Rangers-Islanders and Rangers-Devils games was something I always looked forward to. Every game was always a battle for bragging rights, and the memories I have as a youth weren't as much about the game as they were about leaving the arena and the back-and-forth banter between each team's fans.

Since I live in Queens and commute to and from games on the Long Island Rail Road, heading home from the Garden after a loss to the Islanders was never fun. On the other hand, I was always a little happier leaving MSG after the Rangers won against either the Islanders or Devils than when the Rangers beat another opponent.

Despite the string of nonplayoff seasons, the last home game of the 2003–04 season was far and away my favorite memory of being at MSG. It was Messier's last NHL game—although he hadn't announced he was going to retire at that time—and I was fortunate enough to be selected as one of the "Blueshirts off Our Backs" recipients. However, unlike in other years when the ceremony took place on the ice, it took place in the locker room.

I was given Karel Rachunek's jersey—a defenseman who had been acquired from Ottawa at the trade deadline that season. After I spent a few minutes talking to Rachunek and posing for a picture, I walked past Messier, whose locker was just a few away from Rachunek's. Before I left, I shook Mark's hand and thanked him for the memories. My idol responded with a simple, "Thanks, kid," that I remember to this day.

After the 2004–05 season was canceled due to a lockout, I finally was able to convince my dad to purchase two season tickets. Section 407 became

Michael Rappaport, lifelong Rangers fan and season ticket holder in section 407 (pre-MSG renovation) and currently section 223. (David Perlmutter)

my home away from home, and I created a special bond with many of my fellow Blue Seat members who make up the heart and soul of the Garden faithful.

The first season I had season tickets—2005–06—was a magical one. Not only was I able to go to as many games as I could, but the team turned the corner and began to win. A lot. Some of my favorite memories at the Garden came during that season. I was there to witness the longest shootout in NHL history, a 15-round classic that ended with a circus between-the-legs shot from Rangers defenseman Marek Malik.

I saw the dominance of Jaromir Jagr, who broke the team's single-season records with 54 goals and 123 points. And I saw the emergence of a rookie goaltender who nobody had heard of before the season started. His name: Henrik Lundqvist, and he took Manhattan by storm on and off the ice. And, of course, I saw the Rangers return to the playoffs.

In the years that I've had season tickets, the playoff games are the ones that stand out to me. Each home game was an all-day event, starting with the Rangers fan buses that would cruise around Manhattan a few hours prior to the puck drop. Every night John Amirante would sing the national anthem, which is one staple of the Garden that never gets old, whether it is the regular season or the postseason. But during the playoffs, his voice—accompanied by thousands of white towels waving in the stands—is a sight that sends chills up and down my spine.

The playoffs have provided some of the highest—and lowest points—of my tenure as a fan. One of the lowest points came during Game 4 of the 2011 Eastern Conference quarterfinals against the Washington Capitals. In the day between Games 3 and 4, Washington coach Bruce Boudreau said that MSG wasn't as loud as people made it out to be. When the Rangers opened up a 3–0 lead in the second period, the crowd broke into a chant of "Can You Hear Us?," which was as loud and long as any chant I've heard at the Garden.

However, the Rangers coughed up the three-goal lead in the third period, and then lost on a fluky goal in double overtime. Leaving MSG that night was one of the lowest points I've had, and the feeling was accentuated two days later when the Capitals eliminated the Rangers in Washington.

But the positive memories outweigh the negatives. I vividly remember Game 3 of the 2006–07 Eastern Conference semifinals, when the Rangers trailed the Buffalo Sabres two games to none.

The game went into overtime, and every Rangers fan was on pins and needles knowing that a Buffalo goal would not only end the game but also effectively the series. That nervous tension turned into unbridled joy when Michal Rozsival scored in the waning minutes of double overtime to keep the Rangers in the series.

The 2012 playoffs will always be a source of great memories for me. The Rangers hosted two Game 7s—against the Ottawa Senators and the Washington Capitals—and skated away with a pair of 2–1 victories. But as loud as MSG was on those nights, it couldn't top Game 5 of the series against the Caps.

With the series tied at 2–2 and the Rangers trailing in the final seconds of the game, Brad Richards tied the score with 7.6 seconds left on the clock. The crowd exploded when the puck went in, but I recall that the energy level stayed just as high during the 17-minute intermission between the third period and overtime. When Marc Staal ended the game with a goal early in overtime, the roar of the Garden was one I hadn't heard before.

Through the wins and losses, the one thing that remains constant is the passion and support of Rangers fans. Through thick or thin, the family atmosphere that I've been a part of in the Blue Seats has never wavered.

One example of this came at the end of the 2005–06 season, when the Rangers were about to be swept by the Devils in the first round of the playoffs. It was a tough pill to swallow, but the Blueshirts had put together a season that hadn't been seen in quite some time.

Before the final faceoff was to be taken with four seconds left, the crowd at MSG—starting with the Blue Seats—gave the team a standing ovation, and chanted "Let's Go Rangers" through the final buzzer and the handshake line.

The passion and the unwavering loyalty that I share with so many others are the reasons why I am proud to call myself a Rangers fan and a member of the Garden faithful!

Acknowledgments

Hockey is a game where teamwork is essential. The same holds true in book production.

Like a goal scored by a forward that's produced in tic-tac-toe fashion, the author is the beneficiary of prior digging that includes considerable research and planning. In that regard, considerable thanks are in order for my interns who did the behind-the-scenes grunt work so necessary to get the project on track.

Anything beyond a fervent thanks to Allyson Gronowitz and Michael Rappaport for their assorted help would be like gilding the rose or painting the lily. Like Ryan Callahan, they delivered in the clutch.

Others on the roster made meaningful contributions in one form or another and a deep bow is in order for Jordan Schoem, Darrin Im, Alec Kessler, Jared Lane, Michael Leboff, Ted Lawrence, and Jim Charshafian.

As always, for a project such as this to get over the goal line, a major assist is necessary, and in this case, the Big A goes to Adam Motin, super editor and hockey savant, par excellence!

The following books provided invaluable information in one form or another in researching this book, and I am indebted to the authors for their work: *Tales from the Ranger Locker Room*, by Gilles Villemure; *Andy Bathgate's Hockey Secrets*, by Andy Bathgate and Bob Wolff; *Messier: Hockey's Dragon Slayer*, by Rick Carpiniello; *Battle on the Hudson: The Devils, the Rangers, and the NHL's Greatest Series Ever*, by Tim Sullivan; *Losing the Edge: The Rise and Fall of the Stanley Cup Champion New York Rangers*, by Barry Meisel; *Game of My Life: New York Rangers: Memorable Stories of Rangers Hockey*, by John Halligan and John Kreiser; *When the Rangers were Young*, by Frank Boucher and Trent Frayne; *The New York Rangers: Broadway's Longest Running Hit*, by John Kreiser and Lou Friedman; and *New York Rangers: Seventy-Five Years*, by John Halligan.

In addition, I relied on several of my own Rangers books of yesteryear and *Metro Ice*, the history of New York–New Jersey hockey co-authored with the late, great Tom Sarro. That book, along with my *Those Were the Days*, provided portions of the oral history sections. Ditto for *Where Have You Gone, Hockey Stars?*

I would be remiss if I neglected to offer a posthumous thanks to John Henderson, publisher of *Metro Ice*. John was a longtime Rangers fan—and photographer—who conceived the idea for *Metro Ice* and provided historic photos.

John and Tom are sorely missed as both friends and hockey historians.

Finally, a fervent hunk of thanks to Glen Sather, who has been supportive since his playing days as a Boston Bruin and remains so through the still new century.

Plus, more thanks to his very competent and efficient public relations staff including John Rosasco, Brendan McIntyre, and Dino Ticinelli, who always are friends in need and indeed.

Epilogue
Two Most Emotional Moments, Four Decades Apart

Covering the Rangers, both as a fan—vice president of the Rangers Fan Club in 1953–54—and later as a journalist, I experienced two distinct emotional moments separated by some 40 years. And so, I will end this book with an oral history of my own.

The first moment involved a Rangers game I'll never forget but has long been forgotten by most New Yorkers.

The second was a remarkably emotional moment involving two members of the Blueshirts organization, coach Mike Keenan and goalie Mike Richter. The following stories appear in chronological order.

As emotional hockey nights go, the reunion of two Hall of Famers in Rangers livery was about as unlikely as a cow jumping over the moon, but it did happen on the night of January 20, 1954.

Having watched hockey at two Madison Square Gardens over more than seven decades, I consider the game between the Rangers and the Boston Bruins the most emotion-filled of my life. So let's start at the beginning.

There were 13,463 spectators at the old Madison Square Garden on Eighth Avenue between 49th and 50th streets that night for a reason: the Bentley

Brothers, Max and Doug, would be reunited after their separation as teammates seven years earlier.

The pair, along with Bill Mosienko, had comprised the Pony Line of the Chicago Black Hawks during the mid-1940s and seemed destined to go on forever until the undermanned Chicago sextet dealt Max to Toronto for five regulars during the 1947–48 season.

The deal stunned the hockey world because Max and Doug were considered inseparable. Both players were crushed by the move but adjusted to the trauma. They hoped against hope that one day they would be reunited, but with each year the hope seemed less realistic.

When Doug retired in 1951, the chances of the Bentleys skating together disappeared completely. Max continued to star for the Maple Leafs, while Doug returned to Saskatchewan where he became player-coach of the Saskatchewan Quakers, an affiliate of the New York Rangers. By sheer coincidence, Max, who had finally decided to retire, changed his mind and returned for the 1953–54 season as a member of the Rangers.

At the time he signed Max, Rangers general manager Frank Boucher could not have been thinking about reuniting the grand pair because (a) Boucher had no idea how Max would fare with his lowly Rangers, and (b) Doug had been away from the NHL too long.

Although Max may have lost a half-step since his prime, he was an immediate hit on Broadway. "Our town has its biggest hero in years," wrote columnist Jimmy Powers in the *Daily News*. "Max Bentley is an old pro who brings the Garden crowd to its feet every time he takes the disk in his own zone and starts down the ice with it."

Apart from his unmatched skating agility and sudden feints and swerves, Max's trademark was a galvanic wrist shot. "He developed that shot milking cows on the farm," said Doug. "Milking made his wrists big and strong."

But Max couldn't carry the Rangers alone and there were many times that he sat at the end of the bench with his head hung low and bothered by some ailment. Yet the vintage Max was so impressive that one night a Garden official approached Boucher and wondered about bringing a second Bentley to Manhattan.

"If Max is a sample of what one Bentley can do on that ice," the official told Boucher, "I wish the Rangers had another to go with him. If Doug can stand up, he must be better than most of these kids we've got."

Boucher agreed, in part. He knew that Doug Bentley, in his prime, would be a superb catalyst for the Rangers, but the manager also realized that Doug had only been playing part-time minor league hockey while coaching and was too old and out of shape to be considered.

Or was he?

The more Frank mulled it over, the more he grew convinced it was worth trying. He phoned the owner of the Saskatoon team, which had a working agreement with the Rangers, and said he wanted Doug in New York. The answer was a resounding "No!" By now it was December and the Rangers needed help. Normally a mild-mannered sort, Boucher decided to get tough with the Saskatoon officials and threatened to pull the Rangers-owned players off the team, leaving the Quakers with a skeleton squad. He then tossed in a pacifier: he would replace Doug Bentley with Frankie Eddolls, a former NHL defenseman with some coaching potential. By mid-January of 1954 the Saskatoon officials agreed, and Doug Bentley was told to grab the earliest possible flight to New York.

The thermometer read 40 degrees below zero when Doug climbed aboard the plane at Saskatoon Airport on January 19, 1954. From the start, he had doubts about his decision to try a comeback. "I was only doing spot playing with the Quakers," he said. "On top of that I had been having a bad time with my nerves. I didn't think the NHL would help that condition. That's why I was against the move. But Boucher kept after me and, finally, he offered me the biggest money I ever got in my life, even in my best days with the Black Hawks. The money did it. That and the fact that I knew I could help Max. I could assist him on the ice and help settle him off the ice."

On a Wednesday night, January 20, 1954, the Rangers were scheduled to face the fourth-place Bruins whom New York trailed by two points. Even under the best of circumstances it would not be easy for Doug, but this time there were such added problems as plane connections.

"It was late Tuesday night when we left," said Doug, "and just as we were about to take off I discovered I had left my skates at the Saskatoon Arena. They had to hold the flight while I went back to get them."

Boucher, a former member of the Royal Canadian Mounted Police, had personally flown to Saskatoon to "get his man" and sat alongside Doug as the four-engined propeller craft plied its way east. Neither man slept during the trip, which finally brought them into New York Wednesday at midday. There was ice at the Garden that afternoon so Doug took a practice skate.

By late afternoon on Wednesday, sportswriters carried word that the Bentley brothers would, in fact, be reunited that night against the Bruins. "But," said Doug, "neither Boucher nor Muzz Patrick, the Rangers coach, said a word about what they were going to do with me. So, I figured we'd all play it by ear."

Shortly before game time Patrick and Boucher huddled and eventually decided to place Doug on left wing—his normal position—with Max at center and Edgar Laprade on right wing. Laprade, who was normally a center, had been one of the smoothest, most adroit centers in Rangers history in his prime. But he, too, had aged, had even retired, and, at age 34, was persuaded by Boucher to skate once more. Many Rangers fans were skeptical about Laprade's ability to adjust to his right wing position while skating with the unpredictable Bentleys.

But nobody was as uncertain as Doug Bentley. As he sat nervously twitching his legs in the dressing room before the opening faceoff, Doug wondered why he had ever permitted Boucher to talk him into this crazy stunt. "I was afraid I'd make a fool of myself," the elder Bentley recalled. "I was as nervous as a kitten…must have walked up and down the dressing room at least a hundred times."

At last it was time. Organist Gladys Goodding played "The Star Spangled Banner" and referee Frank Udvari dropped the puck for the opening faceoff. Just as quickly, Doug's doubts disappeared. "It seemed," he reflected years later, "that every time we touched the puck we did the right thing."

Doug scored the game's first goal at 12:29 of the first period on a pass from defenseman Jack Evans. At 15:44 Max set up Wally Hergesheimer for a power-play score against Bruins goalie Jim Henry, then Doug fed Paul Ronty, who gave New York a 3–0 lead. The Bentleys were still in low gear, and before the period ended the Bruins had scored twice to pull within a goal of New York. By this time, though, the crowd knew that it was seeing a re-creation of the Bentley brothers of yesteryear, only the jerseys were different.

"Once the people started to holler for us," said Doug, "I knew that was it. I knew we'd really go. I knew because right off the bat I could tell that Max hadn't forgotten any of his tricks or mine either."

Just past the 6:00 mark in the second period, Patrick sent the Bentleys out again. This time they combined for the brand of razzle-dazzle that earned them both a niche in the Hockey Hall of Fame.

"We criss-crossed a couple of times on our way to their blue line," explained Doug, "then I fed it to Max and he put it right in."

Usually nervous, Max was now beside himself with joy, and when he got to the bench after scoring he draped his arm over his brother's shoulder and said, "Same old Doug. You're skating the same, handing off the same, and fooling 'em the same." Less than two minutes later they skated out and, with radar-like passes, set up Camille Henry for still another Rangers goal. The middle period ended with New York ahead 6–3.

In the third period Wally Hergesheimer scored for the Rangers at 9:59 but the fans clamored for the Bentleys and Patrick acknowledged their cries as the clock reached the 15:00 mark. This time Edgar Laprade shared in their pattern-passing wizardry, which sent veteran hockey writers into fits of gleeful cheering.

"To say that the reunion was a success," said Joe Nichols of *The New York Times*, "is a weak understatement. The Bentleys frolicked like a couple of kids out skylarking."

Flanked by the brothers, Laprade swiftly crossed the center red line, then skimmed a pass to Doug on the left who just as quickly sent it back to Laprade as he crossed the Boston blue line. By now, only one Bruins defenseman was back, trying to intercept the anticipated center slot pass from Laprade to Max speeding along the right side. Laprade tantalized the Boston player, almost handed him the puck, and when he lunged for it Laprade flipped it to Max, who was moving on a direct line for the right goalpost. Laprade meanwhile had burst ahead on a direct line for the left goalpost, ready for a return pass. Both goalie Jim Henry and the defenseman—and possibly even Laprade—expected Max to relay the puck back to Edgar, so Henry began edging toward the other side of the net. Max faked and faked and faked the pass but continued to move toward the goal until, without even shooting the rubber, he calmly eased it into the right corner. Henry stood mesmerized by the Bentley magic. The audience went wild. "It was like a dream," Doug recalled. "Everything we did turned out right."

The final score was 8–3 for New York. Max and Doug had combined for a total of eight points between them—Doug with one goal and three assists, and Max with two goals and two assists. "They put on a display of smooth, smart stickhandling that brought back memories of a supposedly extinct hockey era," wrote James Burchard of the *World Telegram and Sun*. "It was a joy to behold."

So was the dressing room scene, although at first glance you couldn't be sure you were witnessing jubilation. There sat Max, the emotional brother, with tears streaking down his face. "He's crying for happiness," said Doug, who himself was unwinding a few feet away. "He's tickled because we finally played together again…and so am I."

Few had realized that Doug hadn't slept for nearly two days and had also suffered through a dramatic temperature change, traveling from frigid Western Canada to balmy New York. "I'm wringing wet from sweating," Doug commented, "and feel completely bushed. Here it's 80 degrees warmer than in Saskatoon. I've had no sleep. My nerves are shot and I had one of the greatest evenings of my life. You explain it."

Explanations flowed as easily as Bentley goals. "I wasn't surprised at Doug's play," said coach Muzz Patrick. "I've seen him play. I know what he can do. I've been sold on Doug Bentley a long, long time."

Boucher, who had dreamed up the scheme, sat beaming on the trainer's bench. "As good as Max is alone," he noted, "he's twice as good with Doug."

It took a while for Max to regain his composure but when he did the man whose skating style was described as "moving like a scared jackrabbit" analyzed the extraordinary performance. "I don't think any man ever taps the whole reservoir of his strength," Max mused. "Some go through their entire lives and never get the mileage they should. You can work yourself to a frazzle and fall dead on the floor and swear you can't move a muscle. But if someone sets fire to the house you'll find yourself setting a new speed record getting out. This game was like an intoxicating stimulant. As goal after goal whipped in, the whole team worked itself into a frenzy. It was one of those nights; one I won't ever forget."

Only once before had the Bentleys enjoyed such a productive evening: in 1942 when they were in Chicago, Max scored four goals and three assists in one game and Doug had two goals and four assists. But the Bentleys were 12 years younger then and at their peak. Few of the seasoned observers doubted that this Bentley reunion would be a very special classic and many were in tears, just like Max.

"I've been covering hockey since 1928," said Jimmy Powers of the *Daily News*, "and this game, to me, was one of the most thrilling of all time. I know, because at the end I was so hoarse from cheering I couldn't talk."

The veteran columnist was not alone. Most in the audience of 13,463 shared his feelings and others were crying for happiness as well.

I speak firsthand because I was one of them.

To this day I look back at that January evening as the most emotional hockey night since I began following the Rangers!

On a more personal, emotional level, nothing will match the moment when two major figures in the Rangers organization visited my younger son, Simon, in his room at Columbia-Presbyterian Hospital in the summer of 1993.

It should be noted that Simon was a dedicated New York Islanders fan ever since he attended games at Nassau Veterans Memorial Coliseum while I was broadcasting for SportsChannel.

Simon loved hockey, not only as a fan but also as a player, and he was determined to become a goaltender, although the odds were against him. My wife, Shirley, and I enrolled him at Northwood, a boarding (prep) school near Lake Placid, New York, where the headmaster sold us a bill of goods about how much hockey Simon would be playing.

Unfortunately, he was sixth out of six goalies, obtained limited ice time, and gradually grew to dislike Northwood and the extraordinarily frigid 1992–93 winter in Lake Placid (it snowed the June day my wife picked him up after finals, for instance). Still, when he did get to play, it was thrilling because the Northwood varsity team played in the 1980 Olympic rink in downtown Lake Placid.

At least once a month Simon and a friend or two would take a train down to Manhattan on a Friday night and remain with us until Sunday morning,

214 | WE ARE THE RANGERS

when they completed the Amtrak round trip back to Northwood. On the weekend in question, I arranged for Simon & Company to accompany Shirley to the fourth Penguins-Islanders playoff game at Uniondale.

A thoroughly absorbed Islanders fan (he was five when the Isles won their fourth Cup, in 1983), Simon was tickled to see a playoff game and enamored of the manner in which his heroes conducted themselves. Spearheaded by penalty killer Tom Fitzgerald's two shorthanded goals, the Isles rallied for a stirring 6–5 victory that permanently impacted most who viewed the match.

I always enjoyed having Simon at games, but this one was so special and ended so euphorically, I was filled with transports of joy when I got behind the wheel of our Honda and began driving Shirley, Simon, and his friends back to Manhattan. But as I drove, the ecstasy diminished with every mile. From the car's rear, the interior was punctuated by spasmatic coughing that carried right through to my very core.

Simon was hacking away so intensely that I began asking myself whether I should permit him to return to school the next morning. When we arrived back at our apartment, I mentioned my concern to Shirley and we decided we'd wait until the next morning before deciding. The problem, of course, was that Simon had to be up early and at Pennsylvania Station by 10:00 AM to catch the train.

Shortly after he awakened, I suggested that it might be wiser for him to remain in the city and see a doctor on Monday. With typical teenage bravado, he insisted that he'd be okay, that he'd see a nurse (or doctor) in Lake Placid, and not to worry. Because I wanted not to worry and because my wife figured it was all right for him to head north again, I raised no objections.

Later in the week Simon phoned and seemed completely recovered. I remember admonishing myself for being overprotective. Somehow I managed to forget that he had suffered through "walking pneumonia" during the winter and assorted other ailments that we considered ordinary for a growing boy.

Meanwhile, his Islanders went on to defeat Pittsburgh before being eliminated by the Canadiens. School ended in late spring, and Simon returned home to prepare for a summer job as a junior counselor at a day camp near our country home in the Catskill Mountains. He appeared to be perfectly normal. One Saturday morning we went to the beach at Riis Park and played a hard game of paddle handball under a broiling sun. I remarked to myself how well

Simon held up under adverse conditions. But I also recall that when I encouraged him to take a swim with me later, he said he was tired and just wanted to stretch out. No sweat; teenagers like to nap on Saturdays.

But there were other signs that something was wrong with Simon, physically. First, about a week after returning from Lake Placid, he complained of an earache. Our regular doctor checked him out, found mild signs of an ear infection, and recommended an ear, nose, and throat clinic. The prescription didn't work, so we tried another. There were other symptoms but each taken on its own hinted at only a passing ailment. We thought it might be allergies and took him to see our allergist. He noticed a rapid heartbeat at the time but attributed it to the fact that Simon was taking antihistamines, decongestants, and an antibiotic—all of which could mean an elevated heart rate.

One Friday afternoon in late June, Simon—who had been a competitive mountain bike racer, too—and I took a leisurely cycle in Riverside Park, adjoining the Hudson River. Our destination was my cousin Gerry's apartment about two and a half miles away. The sun was bright, the air warm but not overbearing, and the ambience—if you will excuse the expression—swell.

Normally, Simon would speed ahead of me and then circle until I caught up, then take another sprint and wait. This time, he kept pace with me and, to my astonishment, halted and got off his bike after we had pedaled up a rather modest hill. "I need a rest, Dad," he implored.

That seemed strange to me, but after a brief respite we resumed our ride, and, yet again, after another climb, he requested a rest for a few more minutes. Little did I realize that Simon was just a weekend away from suffering heart failure.

On Monday, June 28, the Devils held a press conference to announce a new coach. Simon had had a difficult weekend. His ear continued to bother him and a lethargy overcame him, as did nausea. Shirley was so frustrated over the doctors' failure to isolate any cause for his problems, she didn't know who to contact next. On Sunday night she obtained a prescription for his nausea, and on Monday she scheduled an appointment at Manhattan's Eye and Ear Hospital for another examination.

At approximately the same time Devils president and general manager Lou Lamoriello announced that Jacques Lemaire had been named head coach (to replace Herb Brooks), Simon collapsed in the doctor's office of heart failure.

Unfortunately, nobody knew precisely why he had taken ill, but he was rushed (with Shirley) to St. Vincent's Hospital by an emergency medical service ambulance.

When I phoned home to get messages from my office manager, I was told that Simon was in a hospital—mistakenly named Beth Israel—and "probably had an attack of ulcers."

After regaining my composure, I dashed to my car, along with colleague Steve Viuker, who had accompanied me to the press conference. Ulcers? Simon never had a hint of ulcers but, perhaps, the symptoms were there after all. By the time I returned home, word had gotten through that they were at St. Vincent's. I headed for the subway and spent 20 agonizing minutes riding to the hospital.

Upon arriving in the emergency room, I found Shirley and Simon surrounded by doctors and emergency medical service people. All I could think about was the original message—"a bleeding ulcer"—and wondered what was going on with the procedure.

I was quickly introduced to the EMS people, one of whom was rather corpulent and perspiring profusely. I was able to give Simon a hug and kiss and some measure of reassurance, although I hadn't a clue as to his true condition.

Neither, as I would soon learn, did the pediatric emergency room people at St. Vincent's. The original guess of bleeding ulcers apparently had been discarded almost immediately. They had taken him into the emergency room and immediately decided he was in anaphylactic shock, despite Shirley's attempts to tell them he had been taking the new medications for more than 24 hours and there was no way the kid was in anaphylaxis. Unfortunately, a part of the treatment was pumping him full of liquids, and within moments of my arrival Simon was choking and coughing up pink froth.

At this point the medical crew realized that they were probably killing Simon rather than saving him and they tried to catheterize him (a thin tube inserted up the penis, with no anesthesia) so that they could get the liquid back out of him as rapidly as possible.

It was then that I discovered how brave my son really was under the most excruciating conditions. Not that he laughed off the pain—far from it. But he coped with the trauma of it all with a blend of stoicisim and fortitude that surely surpassed anything I could match under similar conditions.

Twice they tried the catheterization, which they soon decided was two times too many. I think it began to dawn on everybody in the room that Simon—with no previous history of heart problems and a healthy athlete—was somehow, unaccountably, in heart failure.

Suddenly, I remembered that both Simon and his older brother, Ben, had been diagnosed with heart murmurs. But after careful analysis, our pediatrician had determined that both had "systolic," or harmless, heart murmurs, which they might well grow out of (Shirley had had a systolic murmur when she was a child). In both cases it was said to have no relation to future ailments as they grew to adulthood.

After considerable examination it was determined that Simon would be removed to an intensive care unit, where he would be further examined and diagnosed. At this point neither Shirley nor I had any indication that his young life was teetering in the balance, nor did we know what to expect in the next 24 hours.

In the relative security of the intensive care unit, Simon was checked regularly and seemed to feel a bit more comfortable. My main task was ferrying cans of seltzer from the soda dispenser down the hall to his bedside.

A Dr. Lee, who supervised the pediatric ICU, indicated that Simon's condition could improve overnight. That would have been comforting had the doctor known precisely the nature of Simon's ailment at the time, which he didn't. He did, however, ask us questions about whether anyone else had mentioned lately that Simon had an enlarged heart. No one had. He told us that the head of pediatric cardiology, Dr. Liu, would be performing an echocardiogram on Simon soon. In the meantime, Simon was being given several medications, which we had never heard of, intravenously.

Shirley remained overnight at Simon's bedside. I eventually took the subway home, walked Cleo, the Airedale, flopped in bed, and wondered what was going on.

As promised, Dr. Liu performed the echocardiogram and then disappeared for most of the day. Unaware of the details, I returned to St. Vincent's in the afternoon and happened to arrive as Shirley left the ICU for a respite.

Instinctively, I sensed bad news when we embraced, although I never imagined the gravity of Simon's condition. After I hugged Simon, Shirley and I were called aside by Dr. Liu. She clearly did not want to converse in front of Simon and led us to an empty children's playroom. "Your son is very ill," she said. "His heart is in poor condition, almost useless."

It was as if a grenade had exploded in my stomach. *Heart. Useless.* The words resonated uncontrollably, mystifyingly. We're talking about a 15-year-old who had competed in a world cross-country mountain-biking event, who had played a 21-point game of hard paddleball in a noonday sun only weeks ago.

One question kept repeating: how could it be?

But it was, and we sent for a private ambulance to take Simon to what would be his "home" for the next two terrifying months—Columbia-Presbyterian Babies' Hospital.

A pair of pleasant, heavily accented Russian paramedics finally arrived at about 8:00 PM that very hot summer evening (Tuesday, June 29), and loaded Simon (with Shirley) into the rear patient's compartment. I would again take the subway home.

As I helped them aboard, I experienced a doleful feeling that Simon might not survive the night, that I might never see him again. Yet I tried not to betray my thoughts. I put on an encouraging face. "You'll be okay, guy!" I said as the ambulance door closed, and then I returned toward the subway.

Simon had become aware of his deteriorating condition earlier in the day and, somehow, coped with it without any emotional breakdown, although I'm not sure how he managed to do so. He maintained that amazingly strong disposition throughout the ordeal, which began in earnest when he checked into Columbia-Presbyterian and was taken to the pediatric ICU.

We learned that sometime in the past—perhaps a month, perhaps several months before—Simon had suffered a virus, and the virus had reached his heart. The destructive process then began and culminated with the collapse on June 28. By the time he reached Columbia-Presbyterian, Simon's heart was functioning at only 13 percent.

Life became an endless nightmare and the bad news just kept coming. As I look back on it now, I see Shirley and me sitting there, stunned and numb, while the doctors kept rolling out a new litany of horrors. They were wonderful, calm, confident, positive; we were terrified, confused, basically in shock and denial.

Simon's life was in grave danger. But the doctors told us that they had definitely found inflammation in the heart tissue, signs that a virus had once been present. Cautiously, they said they might be able to treat the virus with medicine and restore his heart to a semblance of normalcy. If that didn't work, only a heart transplant would save the lad.

I can't tell you the profundity of the shock of hearing those words: *heart transplant.* It was impossible to take in that they were talking about our son—our skiing, skating, biking, soccer-playing son. It was at almost this precise moment in time that basketball star Reggie Lewis dropped dead on the playing court, of what they later confessed was cardiomyopathy. With what Simon was undergoing at the time, it seemed impossible to label him "lucky." But if he hadn't collapsed in a doctor's office, he probably would have died.

For a week Shirley and I hoped and prayed. For one brief period on a late Friday morning, as they began to withdraw Simon from the medication that kept his heart pumping, we all hoped Simon had beaten the virus, beaten the inflammation. But no, almost to the moment they told us the medication would all be out of his bloodstream, Simon's heart rate skyrocketed and simultaneously his blood pressure began to disappear. Simon's heart was irreversibly, irretrievably, irreparably destroyed. Our son was going to need a heart transplant.

At this point you may be wondering what all this has to do with hockey. In fact, throughout the ordeal—from getting the communiqué at the Lemaire press conference to the start of the new season—hockey people were directly involved in the grieving, waiting, and healing process this hideous event was about to become.

At first, I had decided to keep Simon's condition from all but family and close friends, but word leaked to *Daily News* columnist Bob Raissman, who wrote an oblique item about the hospitalization. I figured if Raissman had the item, I'd better contact my pal, Phil Mushnick, at the *New York Post*, which I did. The hockey community got wind of it when we had to cancel the trip to Boston. Soon, the outpouring of emotion became a bit overwhelming.

A huge card, signed by the members of the U.S. Olympic team, arrived along with good wishes from coach John Cunniff and USA Hockey bigwigs.

At this point, I decided to become more proactive. I figured an appearance by a hockey personality or two might be a tonic for a lad who was weakening by the day. I phoned the Islanders, Simon's favorite team, and learned that all of the players were out of town. Ditto for the Devils, his second-favorite club; they, too, were away. That left me with the Rangers, far from being on my son's hit parade.

When I called the Rangers public relations man, Barry Watkins, he was very understanding. "Mike Richter might be in town," he said, "and maybe even Mike Keenan."

Keenan. I thought for a moment and without hesitation said, "Sure, if you could get either or both, let me know."

I hung up and then I began hesitating. My relationship with Keenan had taken several strange turns ever since our first encounter nearly two decades ago.

One meaningful encounter took place in Toronto at the *Hockey News* annual awards luncheon, of which Keenan was an honoree. I was seated next to Keenan and his wife, Rita, each of whom was an absolutely delightful tablemate.

My affection for Mike grew when I learned that he was a biking enthusiast. We exchanged cycling tales and even vaguely talked of pedaling somewhere together sometime in the distant future. Interestingly, the conversation hardly ever dwelled on hockey, which was fine for all of us.

Keenan was the antithesis of the ogre who had been portrayed by players as "Adolf" (as in Hitler). In my eyes, the most noteworthy aspect of the chat was Keenan's remarkable calm, warmth, and insights. He was so totally unlike his image that I wondered whether he needed a new press agent or if he simply pulled a Jekyll-and-Hyde transformation, depending on the season.

But one summer, as I prepared my annual NHL preview for *Inside Sports* magazine, I wrote a squib about Keenan's club at the time, the Blackhawks. One of my choice morsels suggested that if the dislike-for-Mike atmosphere had any effect, it would cause a tidal wave in Lake Michigan.

The article hit the stands about a week after training camp began, which is when my office phone rang.

"[Blackhawks PR man] Jim DeMaria, Stan." His voice was unusually austere. "Mister Keenan would like to talk to you."

Keenan did not think that line I wrote was very funny. We went back and forth for a while. At one point I believed he simply was trying to intimidate me, and yet at another, I suspected that he was sensitive enough to actually feel hurt by the barb. Who knows? Maybe it was both. I was jolted by the call but also pleased that I hadn't bent to his onslaught.

Years later, when Keenan was appointed coach of the Rangers, I looked forward to a resumption of our relationship—friendship would have been an exaggeration. Now, here I was: Simon was in crisis, Keenan was in town, and I was looking to him for help.

Keenan's persona offered more strength-giving potential than most of the others, and despite our past differences, I thought it would be beneficial if he visited.

What Shirley, Simon, and I needed now was some kind of a family tonic, and it came on a Saturday morning in the form of the two Mikes, Keenan and Richter. The goalie was the first to arrive; quietly gliding in, looking more like a college sophomore than an NHL goalie. He went right over to Simon and handed him a bag filled with Rangers goodies. Richter kidded the kid about not being a Rangers fan and got a broad—yet semisheepish—grin in return.

Richter plopped himself in a big leather chair at Simon's bedside and began chatting with him when another figure appeared in the doorway. I got up to greet the coach, who walked briskly toward the bed, gazing straight at me. Instead of a handshake, he wrapped his arms around me and squeezed the squeeze of a parent who had a special feel for a sick kid. I've been squeezed a few hundred times in my life but none equaled the Keenan hug for a simple message delivery: hang tough, my good friend!

For an hour the two Mikes, myself, Simon, and, later, Shirley, traded stories, exchanged views, and distracted ourselves from the trouble around us. Keenan's demeanor alternated from witty to intensely intellectual as he would carefully explain an aerobic program he thought Simon might try after—we hoped—he obtained his new heart.

Uncannily, we all seemed to realize simultaneously when it was time for the two Mikes to leave. As they headed for the elevator, Keenan spun around and grabbed me a second time. I was inwardly hoping that he would. Shirley and I were terribly anxious about the uncertain days ahead and needed outside reassurance. Mike's hug tightened the emotional vise. If he said anything, I couldn't hear, but I was feeling plenty.

The elevator arrived and they both disappeared through the doors. We returned to the room. "It's enough to make you a Rangers fan," I said to Simon.

He thought for a moment. "Well," he said, "I don't know about that." Spoken like a true Islanders fan, with a fresh reverence for the two Mikes.

I had been so touched by the two visits, I wondered how I could possibly give the two Mikes fair journalistic treatment. Dare I criticize Keenan, who had given me such immense emotional support? Would I ever put the knock on Richter, no matter how badly he played goal?

On Thursday, August 5, a doctor on the cardiology team, Dr. Marianne Kichuk, informed me that the Dibutamine was losing its effectiveness, that Simon would have to be returned to intensive care and placed on another, more potent medicine. Without articulating it, Dr. Kichuk intimated that Simon was dying.

Later, while I tried to relax in the waiting room, Dr. Kichuk walked in and said the precious words: "It looks like a heart is on the way."

It was. When Shirley walked in shortly thereafter, she had obviously been shoring herself up to spend a desolate night with Simon before he went down to PICU for what could be the last time, when she was confronted with a weird scene of what I could only call scared jubilation: a heart was on its way and Simon was being readied for surgery. It would be almost 1:00 AM on Friday, August 6, before he disappeared into the icy operating room.

By 7:00 AM he was in the PICU, tubes and machines all over. But by God, he was already conscious and trying to speak around the respirator and over the medications they had given him to actually paralyze him. Simon's subsequent recovery bordered on the incredible, until he underwent his first attempt to reject the new heart only a week after the transplant. Other complications would occur, but by August 25, Simon Fischler walked back into his own home.

His life never would be the same. He might not ever play goal again, but there was the hope that, despite the many obstacles he would face along the way, he could enjoy a reasonably normal life.

In the meantime, I had hoped to return to a reasonably normal hockey life, although the sense I had was that the ice game never would be the same for me, or for that matter, the NHL.

Over the two decades since the transplant, Simon has experienced a remarkable life while remaining a dedicated Islanders fan.

These days, he does his rooting from the State of Israel, where Simon is married to his lovely wife, Lilach, and has three remarkable children, Odel, nine, Ariel, seven, and Avigail, four. They live on the Kibbutz El Rom in the Golan Heights, only an hour's drive from Metula, home of the Canada Centre, the only Olympic-sized hockey rink in the Jewish State.

The two older kids already have attended the Canada-Israel hockey school, which runs throughout the year in the arena right on the Lebanese border.

By sheer coincidence, Mike Keenan showed up in Metula during the summer of 2013 as coach of Team Canada in the Maccabiah Games, otherwise known as the Jewish Olympics.